Dear Scott,

With abiding
gratitude for your
support of this project
and our common craft.

Collyually

Tom

11/97

A FIELD MANUAL FOR MINISTERS

LOVE MEETS THE
DRAGONS

Tom Owen-Towle

SunInk Publications
37931 Palo Colorado Road, Carmel, CA 93923

DEDICATION

I dedicate this soulful guide on the practical arts of ministry to the student body of the Meadville/Lombard Theological School in Chicago where I spent a most satisfying sabbatical in Fall of 1996. I am especially indebted to the students in my class entitled "Love Meets the Dragons" and to The Rev. Judy Mannheim, my co-teacher, whose contributions enriched this book immeasurably.

TABLE OF CONTENTS

Table of Contents

PROLOGUE

*Our greatest fears are like dragons guarding our
greatest treasures.*

Rumi

Perhaps this is a book better written at the close of my career. Yet while I am still ensconced in the struggle seems
a propitious time to transmit a handful of well-gnarled in-
sights, especially for newcomers entering the gates of this
hallowed and harrowing profession called ministry.

My focus will be upon the beguiling fears, or what I call
the dragons, we clergy encounter in our field. Enticing yet
perilous dragons are endemic to other professions as well, but
I will attempt to address only those swimming the waters of
professional ministry. My thesis is that dragons are the consummate, symbolic beasts that plague ministers and, furthermore, that we are far better off if we attempt neither to slay
nor sidestep but rather to shake hands with them.

Let me begin with my own ministerial journey, a steady
tussle between persistent confidence and nagging doubt. **Love
meets the dragons** is the phrase that most aptly describes my
particular evolution as a person and a professional.

I entered this world ardently wanted by parents who were
in their 30s. I have since believed, even in the gloomiest of
hours, that I possessed ontological "okayness," and that it was
good I was alive. While negotiating life's vicissitudes as well
as countless travesties of my own doing, I have been upheld
by a replenishable pool of hope. No wonder I have ripened
into an unrepentant universalist.

I am a peculiar blend of my folks, Mary and Harold. Mary,
the pensive wordsmith, tireless caregiver, and Presbyterian
church pillar, the likes of which parish ministers plead for: a
trustworthy institutionalist braced with a social conscience.
It was Mom who intuited that ministry and her son might

be a solid match, even when I was too young to spell Jeremiah, let alone Octavius Brooks Frothingham. I have never quite known whether God, my mother, an inner hunger, or some mysterious mix called me into ministry at the age of ten, but it hasn't mattered much, for even in times of confusion and disgruntlement, I've tried to remain faithful to all three sources.

Harold was a born entertainer and good enough to perform with the big bands of his era, but that was too unstable a vocation for one interested in marriage and family. So Dad toiled day and night selling insurance, while his passion sounded forth only occasionally. He overworked and underplayed, marching dutifully to the office until two months before he died, on Christmas eve, nearly 82 years old. To borrow words from Jim Croce's song, "I'm living the dream he kept hid." In truth, my showman spark has caught fire since my Dad died. Whenever I open my belly now in song, it's as if I am crooning for the two of us.

While Dad never fathomed my exuberance for imponderables, he beamed with conspicuous pride whenever his son approached the pulpit and would sneak glances into my printed sermons while sitting on the john late at night. While Mom might shyly mention my books to relatives, Dad would shamelessly peddle them to strangers. So, what do you get when you cross an entertainer with marketing instincts and a social worker who loves literature? Well, in my case, you got a parish minister!

I also extend an overflowing cup of love to our four adult children: Chris, Jenny, Russ, and Erin, who, through our awkward, painful, and triumphant blending as a family, have bountifully affirmed my vocation as well as their mother's, who is also a minister. Despite my foibled fathering, our bond is constant and runs deep.

Emerson called ministry "the first office in the world," yet what has come clear to me at 55 years of age is the conviction that I am not the least bit interested in ranking my various professions of family, ministry, partnership, personal life, and citizenship. All five summons are crucial to heed, and my pilgrimage is most consecrated when I am somehow juggling these life-calls simultaneously!

Words cannot adequately express the love I hold for my wife, Carolyn. The core of my existence dwells in our commitment to muster lives of affection and respect, at work and home. When we were married 24 years ago, we chose relational justice as the governing motif by which to guide our marriage, and, though at times we have fallen short, we've never abandoned our theme.

Back to my ministerial evolution. When the youth minister, Walt Robie, arrived in town, we were blessed with a sage yet playful adult companion. He allowed us youngsters to romp through the bowels of the church basement and tear up the front lawn playing touch football. He even visited me in my sickbed one afternoon, a rare gesture in those days. Impressed by his heartfelt, kindly ministry, I thought to myself, "Wow, I'm not sure there is anything more wonderful in the whole world than what Reverend Walt does! Maybe I could try it someday!"

So, during my teens, I tagged along with the senior minister on shut-in-visits, engaged in theological bull sessions, and delivered testimonies around church campfires or during Sunday services. I remember my talks as being crammed with syrup and piety but, if truth be told, I'm an incorrigible sentimentalist, and my most authentic sermons still emanate from the moister regions of my soul. In my youth I never veered far from the Christian model of being good, doing good, and looking good—a condition that reminds one of Thoreau's lament on his deathbed, "Oh, what demon possessed me that I behaved so well!"

Unlike the life-veterans who enter ministerial training today at the average age of 40, I was a tenderfoot attending San

Francisco Theological Seminary fresh out of Swarthmore College. For the first time my mind cut loose, and I contributed brash poems and defiant essays to our radical seminary journal that got me into hot water with my local, more conservative Southern California Presbyterian church. They even called a board meeting back home to censure their "golden boy" for his incipient heresies. My maddeningly cheerful theology was being severely shaken.

It was the 1960s, and fifty of us seminarians traveled by bus from San Francisco to Selma to heed Martin Luther King, Jr.'s countrywide call to join in civil rights' solidarity. It was my introduction to the South. During the daytime we cleared the fields of cow dung and prepared a campsite for the marchers arriving at dusk. In the evening we joined in rousing rallies led by the likes of Dick Gregory and Peter, Paul, and Mary.

The final day we all marched into Montgomery, singing and holding hands while being cursed at and spat upon by hate-filled crowds along the road. Never in my life had I experienced such feverishly hopeful and hostile emotion jammed together...not until that day I strode alongside sisters and brothers into Montgomery, trying, as Andrew Young exhorted us, "to love the hell out of Alabama!"

Subsequently, what I recall most about my being grilled in 1970 before the Unitarian Universalist ministerial fellowshiping committee in Seattle was being stopped cold by one member's nasty yet utterly germane query, "Well, Tom, you seem like a capable, good enough guy. But how does your theology deal with evil?" I fumbled forth some response at the time, but I have been tormentingly occupied with that question ever since, from Selma to Seattle to San Diego, where my wife and I have co-ministered since 1978. My ministry has been a clumsy, often spineless, yet dogged effort to love the hell out of my own soul, much less that of society.

Love meets the dragons.

Remember the story of the Mariners' charts in the 16th century that outlined rather crudely the shoreline of Europe and Africa? Out there in the Atlantic, where few had yet ventured, mapmakers filled in the uncharted spaces with the words, "Here be Dragons that devour explorers!"

In fact, Irish monks in the Dark Ages would sometimes be set adrift, literally, in frail, little crafts with modest provisions and a few stars to guide them, hoping to land somewhere as missionaries, but realizing they were just as likely to drown. Well, that's what it feels like as we ministers navigate the frightening depths of the humongous ocean trying to elude the dragons of the sea.

The evaluational committee in Seattle was warning me to respect the fearsome mythical beasts of the deep, fully aware that we clergy, however bright or vigilant, are sometimes swept overboard, swallowed up by dragons lying in wait along the waterways of our ministries. They were cautioning me never to take for granted that clergy can sail unscathed around our worlds and not be lost "over the edge." Out of the original 54 candidates who came in with my class in 1970, only a dozen remain in the ministry today. The dragons are real, intractable, and oh, so very complicated.

Dragons are wilier than the Devil (remember Genesis 3:1 states that "The serpent was more subtle than any other beast of the field which Yahweh God had made"). Dragons are incurably ambiguous: formidable and scary yet appealing, enchantingly colorful too. In our Western world mythology, they rigidly symbolize implacable fiendishness; hence, like St. George, we ministers are trained to race forth and slay them. But in Eastern lore dragons are beneficent animals who guard the emperor's throne.

Despite my early, unformed concept of ministry as a frontal assault on blatant evil, my chosen profession as I know it today is incorrigibly taoist, yin and yang, an inexplicable intertwining of joyful ferocity. Oh, how we ministers wish that our profession were neatly contested between angels and demons. What we've inherited instead is an infuriatingly puzzling vocation brimming with dragons that charm and torment. As the medieval mystic Rumi put it: "Our greatest fears are like dragons guarding our greatest treasures."

During my 30 years in ministry, I've been damn near swallowed by some dragons, slain a few by chance or grit, and sidestepped still others. Yet central to this strange and ancient profession has been learning how, as the Chinese would say, to "shake hands" with the majority of my ministerial fears. I wish I could have "purged the land of monsters" (the literal meaning of *catharsis*), but that just isn't achievable. I usually settle for peaceful co-existence.

Here are a few of the shrewd dragons that continue to pester me. Others will emerge throughout the book.

One stubborn dragon is my reluctance to be a troublemaker within or beyond the walls of my parish. I need to match softness of heart with resoluteness of conscience, especially in front of strong women and men who might disagree with, even reject, me.

There is the dragon called "messiah complex" that has pestered me from the start. I'm a giver by nature. I entered the ministry to serve, if not transform people, and have always flirted with an overweening savior-drive.

Another dragon emerges from the brine through my slowness to receive ministry from my parishioners: their authentic caring without having to reciprocate and their honest criticism without having to defend. It requires adroitness to maintain a thick but uncalloused skin as a minister. Laurence Olivier was in a play early in his career that was a royal flop and roundly criticized. Charlton Heston inquired: "I guess you just have to forget the negative reviews, huh?" Olivier snapped back: "On the contrary, we gain more from criticism; we must learn how to forget all the rave reviews!"

Then there's the infuriating two-headed beast that keeps my ministry yo-yoing between being a hermit and being a knight, being judgmental and being appreciative, being weak-kneed and being intrepid.

Dragons abound in my preaching as well. As a child I was exceedingly shy and seldom spoke until I entered kindergarten. Consequently, I had to outgrow my terror of speaking through risking oratory contests in high school. Then I had to confront my fear of making mistakes while preaching during my tenure in Iowa. The dominant challenge in my current preaching nudges me to quote others less and harvest more directly from my own soul. A related dragon is speaking more freely and less text-bound.

My dread of falling flat in front of crowds has diminished since childhood but not disappeared. I guess I'll never be totally relaxed in the pulpit, nor do I really want to be, but I would settle for shaking firmer and less sweaty hands with the uncivilized dragons roaming my soul.

The quip goes that most Americans, clergy included, are even more afraid of public speaking than of death, so speaking at one's own memorial would apparently pose the ultimate terror. Yet, I suspect that silence intimidates a lot of ministers even more than any verbal gaffe.

My sabbatical month utterly alone and quiet in the woods seven years ago was terrifyingly transformative. Intentionally without portfolio—causes to serve, people to assist, or wisdom to proclaim—I forced myself to explore the mysterious cubbyholes of my interior castle. Moreover, I could not avoid facing that dragon guarding the entrance to the ultimate darkness, death.

The scaly dragon called "avoidance," replete with crested head and enormous claws, arises whenever I show preferential treatment to the "weighty," pleasant members of my congregation over the difficult, "peripheral" ones. And I dare not forget the dragon of dependency—that seductive creature embodied in the disturbing Zen question, "Am I helping others because they need help or do they need help because I am helping them?" When my ministry mixes up being a care*taker* with being a care*giver*, all sorts of dragons run amok.

Dragons show up at rites-of-passage too. Why am I reluctant to refer couples to counseling when they aren't ready for marriage? And when officiating as a ritual leader, I sometimes fail to distinguish between tears born of authentic, spontaneous sentiment and crying stirred by my own unresolved feelings.

Additionally, there exists the dragon that tempts me to razzle-dazzle parishioners, perhaps especially colleagues, rather than speak plainly; the dragon that preoccupies me with my own indispensability; the dragon that keeps me from addressing a topic because there are those in my flock who know more about it than I; the dragon that keeps me preaching on pet peeves, or ranting and raving about some "holy cause" without personally demonstrated effort to effectuate change; the dragon that lures me to concentrate upon my strong suits while shirking my "growing edges"; the dragon that keeps my theology secure, my politics closed, and my ethics stiff; the dragon that has me substituting frenzy for fervor; and the dragon that fools me into thinking that prayer, dance, and song are extraneous rather than germane to my spiritual bearing.

Oh, the dragons keep on coming...from sea and land, sky and soul!

Well, so it goes. I might have settled for a more agreeable yet shallow ministerial career, if I hadn't been goaded at the start by a colleague to examine life's dragons. Furthermore, my ministry would have surely stumbled, probably stalled, without the embrace of Love—both human and divine—that graced me at birth, has surrounded me since, and will never let me go, "rest assured."

My life—my ministry: love meets the dragons!

LOVE MEETS THE
DRAGONS

THE CALL

I used to think freedom meant doing whatever you want. It means knowing who you are, what you are supposed to be doing on this earth, and then simply doing it.

Natalie Goldberg

I have a business card now. Finally figured out what to put on it. One word. FULGHUM. That's my occupation. And when I give it away, it leads to fine conversations. What I do is to be the most Fulghum I can be. Which means being a son, father, husband, friend, singer, dancer, eater, breather, sleeper, janitor, dishwasher, bather, swimmer, runner, walker, artist, writer, painter, teacher, preacher, citizen, poet, counselor, neighbor, dreamer, wisher, laugher, traveler, pilgrim, and on and on and on. I and you, we are infinite, rich, large, contradictory, living, breathing miracles—free human beings, children of God and the everlasting universe. That's what we do.

Robert Fulghum

3

Do not seek too much fame,
but do not seek obscurity.
Be proud.
But do not remind the world of your deeds.
Excel when you must,
but do not excel the world.
Many sages and crones are not yet born,
many have already died.
To be alive to hear this song is a victory.

Traditional, West Africa

*The words **car** and **career** come from carrera, the Latin word for racetrack. This suggests that a car and a career both have you going in circles rapidly and competitively.*

William May

*Calling comes from the Latin **vocatio** (vocation), from **vocate** (to call) which was defined by a seventeenth century Puritan divine as 'that whereunto God hath appointed us to serve the common good.'*

William Sloane Coffin

Whatsoever thy hand findeth to do, do it with thy might.

Ecclesiastes 9:10

SOURCES OF MINISTERIAL CALL

*Before **whom** are you destined to give account of your gifts?*

Ancient rabbinic text

It matters not who initiates the onset of the call, or even when it occurs, but to be a full-fledged invitation, we must ultimately render full account of our gifts before three reviewers: God, self, and the larger community. If we are called by God, without passionate confirmation from our own beings, then the call will languish. If we are called at the behest of only internal urge without divine undergirding, it will turn egocentric. Finally, if our call is unresponsive to the cries of society, then, although sustained by inner will and transcendent claim, it will prove vacuous. Frederick Buechner phrases the ministerial call compellingly: "To find our Calling is to find the intersection between our own deep gladness and the world's deep hunger, that point which allows for our fullest expression even as it provides an avenue for our greatest service."

In screening candidates for the ordained ministry, the distinction must be drawn between those who are ready to express their being through the ministry and those who are hungrily trying to discover their identity therein. Prospects are oft-tempted to ground their call in private, unfulfilled psychosocial needs. I grow wary of people who say they are "following their bliss." It sounds presumptuous and self-focused.

Potential ministers must honestly answer the question: "In pursuing the ministry what am I running from?" Some of us are running from a sense of inadequacy or lack of stature, others from loneliness. In truth, most of us entering the ministry are running *from* something; the key is for our evolving ministries to end up running *toward* worthy visions. As James Thurber put it: "All people should learn before they die what

5

they are running to and from and why."

GROWING INTO OUR CALL

Ministers declare a strong **Yes** to God's invitation, the interior yearning, and society's cry. If we don't respond affirmatively to all three sources, then no honorable covenant can be struck. If we respond too quickly, before our answer has matured, then the connection can fray. For example, those of us who felt called into ministry in our pre-teen years must have our early summons consistently validated along our pathway.

But the truth is that no one enters seminary as a full-blown parson. Everyone must do some growing into their ministerial call. Our initial call-and-response will be revisioned and renegotiated throughout our entire lifetime. Alas, too many women and men arrive dreamy-eyed at theological school and feel they are home free. Hardly. Academics are essential in providing the building blocks needed for ministry, but they are insufficient predictors of future ministerial effectiveness.

The likely time when calls are validated is during field work or an internship. In San Diego, we have been a "teaching congregation" for over a decade, and occasionally during the course of their on-the-job training with us, interns have decided to pursue another professional course than ministry. That's an encouraging sign. The internship should assist prospective ministers in discerning the pluses and minuses of both their ministerial desire and appropriateness. The fact is that just as one is called *into* ministry, you can equally be called *out* of it, at any stage along the journey.

Ministry is essentially a practical rather than a theoretical art and needs to be confirmed in the field. I was stretched intellectually, spiritually, and prophetically during my own formative ministerial schooling, but it was the concomitant field work in local churches that matured my call to ministry. Carl

6

Jung's advice reminds seminary students to "learn your theories well, but put them aside when you touch the miracle of the living soul."

When I attended theological school in the early 60s, my fellow seminarians were all males but one, and uniformly in their early-to-mid-twenties. Now, with the massive influx of both women and second-career persons pursuing ministerial training, seminaries are the beneficiaries of persons who are more mature. Jesus provided a comparable example: a lengthy incubation period followed by a shorter tour of duty, serving but three years after preparing for thirty. If the challenge of ministry is to shrink the dissonance between ministerial promise and performance, both congregations and the larger community will surely benefit from older, more life-seasoned ministers.

However, the call to ministry, at any age, is never perfect or pure. That should hardly come as a surprise, since all of the important covenantal calls of human existence—from partnership to parenting to professional life—are beset with doubts amidst our assurance. However, beneath any gnawing anxiety and uncertainty should reside a sufficiently strong and evolving Yes—an affirmation that ministry is the right livelihood for one—"right" as in just and suitable.

Nonetheless, for most of us in ministry, some modicum of ambivalence will remain the order of our day. Clergy must hold together a staggering array of practical and philosophical paradoxes without flying apart. We must be as wise as serpents and gentle as doves. We must be careful not to step on the same toes two weeks in a row. We must know how to raise both money and spirits, week in and week out.

Rabbit Yitzhak of Vorki once took his two sons to see his teacher, Rabbi Bunam, who gave each of them a glass of bock beer and asked them what it was. The elder boy said: "I don't know." Menahem Mendel, the younger, said: "Bitter and good." "This one will become the leader of a fine congregation," said Rabbi Bunam. The taste and substance of ministry will undoubtedly prove to be more like bock beer than not: both bitter and good.

One of my toughest but most helpful seminary professors conveyed an additional sobering reality. He would press us: "If you can do anything else other than ministry, then you probably ought to do it. Ministry is often an underpaid and under-appreciated profession, inordinately demanding, always filled with confusions and conflicts. But if you can't stay away from it, then give yourself fully to it, since it's probably the right livelihood for you!" That admonition properly bumped numbers of my peers into other, equally valid and valuable, callings, while helping some of us see our way clear to stick it out in ministry.

Often clergy are beleaguered by persistent feelings of inadequacy and guilt. We are harassed by a few undermining parishioners and overwhelmed by ministry's perennially unsolvable burdens. When that pall descends, our good clear thinking stops, and we need to remind each other as fellow clergy that it is all right to feel those feelings. They aren't our total reality, and they are offset by a fresh dose of loving acceptance from our friends, within and beyond the parish, fortified by a recommitment to our ministerial call.

Colleague Barbara Pescan offers sage counsel in the throes of such discouragement:

> *Seek the company of people who have a zest for living. Seek also the company of people who cherish you and do not think it too bold to tell you so, clearly and often. Don't hang out with people who are always telling you that the world is in terrible shape. That's simply obvious. Hang out with people who tell you good news too.*

At the end of a brilliant concert, singer Holly Near said she sometimes started feeling very grim about racism, torture, nuclear power, sexism, ecological havoc, and more. Then her brother smiled at her, gave her a hug and said cheerfully, "Yeah, Holly, so what else do you choose to do with your life?"

CALLED TO SPREAD GOOD NEWS

Good news; but if you ask me what it is, I know not; it is a track of feet in the snow, it is a lantern showing a path, it is a door set open.

G. K. Chesterton

Salvation is the issue. I work to produce stories that save.

Toni Cade Bambara

That's what we're here for: to make the world new. We know what to do: seek justice, love mercy, walk humbly, treat every person as though she were yourself. These are not complicated instructions. It's much harder to decipher the directions for putting together a child's tricycle than it is to understand these. Nor are the behaviors they require alien to our habits and desires.

Nancy Mairs

Ministry, contrary to popular notions, is neither a call to self-abnegation nor a call to self-enhancement. Ministry beckons us to be sacrificial without becoming martyrs, enterprising without turning puffy. In a cogent book entitled *Ambition in Ministry: Our Spiritual Struggle with Success, Achievement and Competition*, Robert Schnase draws critical distinctions between destructive and constructive ambition:

Without ambition among its pastors, the church withers and dies. On the other hand, pastors engulfed by ambition kill our most vital witness...That tension is an inescapable feature of ministry, and from this tension can come life and growth.

9

Ministry is the call to serve and spread the gospel, the *evangel*, the good news. Such news will be variously described by different world faiths, and each minister must claim, then proclaim, their own personalized version of "good tidings." My gospel dwells upon giving back love toward the creation that brought us unmerited life. We cannot *repay* the Creator, but we can *respond* with gifts of justice-making and joy-sharing. Such responsiveness constitutes the soul and substance of my ministry.

Marcus Aurelius, the Roman statesman and stoic philosopher (a saintly monarch if there ever was one), put it succinctly in A.D. 121: *"What is your trade? Goodness."* Aurelius meant that our vocation should be quintessentially one of goodness regardless of the particular field in which we labor. Accountant, physician, parent, machinist, or minister, we all answer one fundamental, underlying call: the call to goodness. Aurelius goes on to say: "Let us put an end, once and for all, to this discussion of what a good person should be, and be one."

The Hebrew prophet Isaiah's words (61:1-2) capture the heart of the ministerial mission:

> *The Spirit of the Lord God is upon me, because the Lord has anointed me to bring good tidings to the afflicted; he has sent me to bind up the brokenhearted, to proclaim liberty to the captives, and the opening of the prison to those who are bound, to proclaim the year of the Lord's favor, and the day of vengeance of our God, to comfort all who mourn...*

However phrased, the minister's gospel centers not just upon *information*, but eminently on the *reformation* of society and the *transformation* of soul. Another thing to keep in mind is that whereas Jesus often said, "Be of good cheer," he never used the Aramaic equivalent of "cheerio." We would follow suit in uncovering and promoting **good,** not syrupy, news.

It is certainly imprudent, perhaps impossible, to sustain a vital ministry without a substantive gospel, a redemptive message that delivers joy and sustains justice, liberates humanity and serves the whole of creation.

LIEBEN UND ARBEITEN

When you work you are a flute through whose heart the whispering of the hours turns to music. To love life through labor is to be intimate with life's inmost secret. All work is empty save when there is love, for work is love made visible.

Kahlil Gibran

One of Sigmund Freud's keenest contributions was his insight that our two primary human needs are *lieben und arbeiten*—"to love and to work." They are often inseparable, since I love myself and others most when thoroughly engrossed in creative and compassionate work. Likewise, when I am most fulfilled in my vocational journey, my affectional bonds are nourished as well.

I have known moments when my work and my love lives have interfered with each other, especially when I have tried to garner excessive acceptance through my work or through parishioner ties rather than having my central intimacy needs met at home with partner and family. It has been aptly said: "Nothing can excuse the minister for neglecting the inner circle for the larger circle outside. The welfare of the minister's family comes first." The dragon of sexual misconduct is often only a closed door, a desolate moment, or a power-grab away.

Another perversion occurs whenever I love my work not passionately but compulsively. I, as my father before me, and like so many ministers, am a recovering workaholic. Love and work are mutually reinforcing yet distinct realities to be confused at great personal and professional peril.

I will not presume to offer a slick formula for locating someone else's right livelihood. Discovering our holy art and employing our total selves is one of the trickiest and most personal things we ever do. It involves listening hard to God's range of life imperatives, assessing the universe and society to find out precisely where we can fit in and be used, while, at the same time, becoming ourselves. We are fortunate indeed when our livelihood creates joy, exults in beauty, and delivers compassion to a world hankering for all three.

As the Eastern sages say: "Many paths will take you halfway up the mountain. Only *your* path will take you to the top." We ministers and laity alike must discern the path that is peculiarly ours to travel, and then be bold enough to walk it. There is a profession, even different professions at discrete stages in our journey, waiting for each of us to exclaim: "Yes, that's my call, and I will answer it affirmatively!"

Yet all too frequently in modern times, women and men are inadequately employed, both financially and spiritually. We never find that vocation where there is a genuine intersection between our peculiar gifts and the needs of the world. Then, most of life's satisfaction must happen outside work—through hobbies, family life, and community service.

Our purpose as religious beings, whether at play or work, worship or service, is to help increase the odds of love flourishing in our one and only cosmos. We declare what we believe to be the meanings of the universe by the ways we employ this one brief lifetime.

A HIGH AND HOLY PROFESSION

Having both entered and left the parish ministry against my inclinations, I pay my tribute to the calling, firm in the conviction that it offers greater opportunities for both moral adventure and social usefulness than another calling if it is entered with open eyes and a consciousness of the hazards to virtue which lurk in it. I make no apology for being critical of what I love. No one wants a love that is based upon illusions, and there is no reason why we should not love a profession and yet be critical of it.

Reinhold Niebuhr

William Ellery Channing believed ministry was "the highest human vocation." Ministry is truly a high and holy vocation, not because it places anyone above anybody else; in fact, if anything, ministry sets us alongside our neighbors as companions. It is high and holy because it places humans in direct communion with all that is majestic and worthy. It is high and holy because it can lift us out of despond or bondage and release us for life abundant. It is high and holy because it exhorts us to co-create a society that is politically just, ecologically sustainable, and spiritually satisfying. It is a high and holy calling because it is shared by professionals and laity alike.

I am partial to the term *vocation* or calling with respect to ministry. I also see value in the word *occupation*, because in ministry one's soul is grandly occupied and fulfilled. Ministry is also a *profession*: a post where one is enabled to profess one's deepest convictions and dearest aspirations.

There are three universal reminders on how to keep ministry a high and holy calling: stay *mindful*, stay *laughing*, and stay *collaborating*.

First, holy work embraces the underrated Zen Buddhist virtue of mindfulness. Ministry is inundated with "distractions," which literally means "to be drawn in different directions, to be pulled asunder." Distractions wrench apart. As Bonnie Friedman notes, the word also meant then as it does now, "to pull someone from his or her actual destination." Solid ministry must stay grounded and focused upon its governing gospel and mission. Inevitably, there will be distractions, but they cannot derail clerics who, in alignment with the African-American exhortation, are urged to "keep their eyes on the prize."

Religious essayist Henri Nouwen tells the story of meeting an older experienced professor at Notre Dame where they were both teaching. "And while we strolled over the beautiful campus, he said with a certain melancholy in his voice: 'You know, my whole life I have been complaining that my work was constantly interrupted, until I discovered that my interruptions were my work.'"

Mindfulness also refers to the art of staying attentive to every task within our calling, no matter how menial or insignificant the job might appear. The mindful minister recognizes that God dwells in the ordinary moment more often than the grandiose event.

The core of ministry does not transpire during the dramatic affairs of preaching and community action so much as in unassuming, daily exchanges with parishioners and strangers, in squarely engaging pesky administrivia, in creating the context within which a beloved community can flourish. Like it or not, meetings are one staple of a minister's vocational diet. The trick is to make meetings not merely times when business is transacted but encounters where individual lives are potentially changed, as occasions for the marvelous to transpire amidst the mundane.

There is a humorous repartee from comic writer Roy Blount that relates to ministers as meeting-attenders. Blount mused: "I am just not the kind of person who feels right about calling himself a writer. I mean, I'll bet that Jesse James, when asked what his line of work was, never could bring himself to say, 'Well, I'm a desperado.' He probably said, 'Oh, something in trains.' So, following Blount's thought process, when asked what my line of work is, I am currently prone to say "Oh, something in meetings!"

Stan Kenton, the brilliant jazz musician, once responded

brusquely to a frustrated young band member who was bone-weary of all the scut work and boring travel necessary to being a professional performer. Kenton said: "Hey, quit whining. Remember you aren't paid for blowing your saxophone. You are primarily paid for making the bus rides!" That's it, we clergy are paid not so much for our "stirring" sermons but for the tedious meetings that often generate the personal confidence and sufficient resources to keep a religious enterprise going where sermons of varying quality can be accommodated.

Second, holy work also requires ministers to keep an active sense of humor. Laughter is ministry's saving grace. As George Bernard Shaw reminds us: "Ever-deeper wisdom and ever-broader compassion; laughter lubricates the job." Without laughter, ministers quickly turn into joyless crusaders. We are called to be serious without turning grim. Although humor is integral to our species, it doesn't reach full fruition until cultivated. Nearly seventy years ago William Austin Smith judiciously recommended:

> *Every Divinity School might well have in its senior year, along with courses in systematic divinity and homiletics, a course in the great masters of comedy, and to arouse our sluggish wits and keep us on our guard, it might not be amiss to carve upon our pulpits, side by side with the lean Gothic saints, the figures of Aristophanes or Moliere with warning finger.*

Laughter keeps ponderous ministerial challenges in perspective. It diminishes our susceptibility to attacks of inadequacy. One of the greatest dragons facing ministers is scrambling to reach the "perfection" we seek and many parishioners expect. As Methodist minister Pierce Harris puts it:

> *The modern parson has to make as many visits as a country doctor, shake as many hands as a politician, prepare as many briefs as a lawyer, and see as many people*

15

as a specialist. They have to be as good an executive as the President of a university, as good a financier as a bank CEO, and in the midst of it all, they have to be such good diplomats that they could umpire a baseball game between the Knights of Columbus and the Ku Klux Klan... There is no way any single human being can live up to all these expectations.

Yet, the New Testament urges us to be whole not perfect (*teleios*) persons, replete with strengths and flaws. As one of my early ministerial associates reminded me: "Even Confucius and Jesus had their bad days." In the midst of inevitable ministerial turmoil and trials we are summoned to forego perfection but pursue progress, to be mindful of one's call to serve not save. The burden of ministry grows unwieldy unless lightened by the healing gifts of humor and playfulness.

Third, ministry becomes high and holy work whenever we acknowledge that ours is a covenantal enterprise. The defining quality of effective ministry is its cooperative nature. One ought never to minimize the imaginative notions clergy produce in solitude; nonetheless, our work comes fully alive when linked with countless others, known and unknown, from near and far.

We never work alone, and we must recognize sisters and brothers in whose debt our profession stands, those who have paved the way for us, others coming after us, and individuals who are the current beneficiaries of our vocational gifts and wounds, be they laity or other religious professionals. Holy work is not a *solitary* but a *solidary* enterprise. Authentic ministry consists of personal convictions, transformed into commitments, shared with companions, and embodied in community. Pulpit and pew need to share the burdens and glory, the credit and blame. Ministry is irrevocably a partnered reality.

Laity and clergy are yoked as peers in its ancient meaning of camaraderie. We are colleagues in that we are leagued in alliance with one another through pursuing a common end.

Whether laity and clergy are called accomplices, partners, peers, or colleagues, it matters not; what is critical is that we create and incarnate a shared vision together. As Episcopalian priest Carter Heyward phrases it:

> This power to create justice, to make right relation, to sustain mutuality, and to make amends when we fail is sacred power. It is the power of God, ours insofar as we share in it. We do not god alone. We bear sacred power in our connectedness with the whole creation.

Lamentably, ministry has all too often been a Lone Ranger operation, fit for egotists and soloists. We talk about *my* instead of *our* ministry. The dragon of possessiveness gnaws on us. Yet ministry at its truest remains a shared partnership not unlike marriage wherein pew and pulpit pledge their troth, for better, for worse, through sickness and health. The fact that there are divorces and remarriages in partnership as well as ministry does not dilute the power and promise integral to both.

In the novel *Heaven Help Us* by Herbert Tarr, the veteran seminary dean who preaches at Rabbi Gideon Abel's installation offers this wisdom to the gathered congregation:

> Though he is a person of dedication and kindness, intelligence and good humor, Rabbi Abel cannot serve you if you do not assist him. Your rabbi is not a soloist, and you are not his audience; he is not a professional Jew, and you are not amateurs. But together you are a holy congregation.

So may it come to pass in our parishes!

THE COMMISSIONS

M inistry is composed of tasks, or what I call "commissions"—responsibilities that have been assigned by
powers and history beyond merely our own personal predi-
lections. *Commission* literally means "something sent with,"
and indicates that productive, fulfilling ministries are summoned and sent forth with directives and prayers. We do not
commission ourselves; we are commissioned.

For Christian ministers there abides the unwavering connection with "The Great Commission" delivered by Jesus at
the close of Matthew. The Nazarene commissioned his followers to go forth into the world and "make disciples of all nations, baptizing them in the name of the Father, and of the
Son and of the Holy Spirit, and teaching them to observe all
that I have commanded you. I will be with you always, to the
end of time." This quintessential commission, coupled with
its reassuring promise, can inspire and guide all vocational

responsibilities assumed by a minister.

The American psychologist Erik Erikson taught that mature persons will develop "the capacity to commit him or herself to concrete affiliations, to abide by such commitments, even though they call for significant sacrifice." Such is certainly the case with ministry. It simply does not exist without being commissioned, without live congregations, without an historical tradition, without divine imperative, without societal challenges. We don't minister in the abstract, or at large, but serve in particular locations during a given era through tangible encounters with individuals and groups. One of Lily Tomlin's bizarre characters said: "When I was growing up, I always wanted to be somebody. Now I realize I should have been more specific!" Or as Ralph Waldo Emerson phrases it: "God has need of a person here." Not just anywhere, but in this special spot.

The amorphousness of ministry is heightened whenever one refers to it as "one of the last general practices." To be sure, ministry encompasses an inordinate range of duties: from administration to teaching, from fund-raising to being a spiritual guide. But clergy ought not be conceived of as "the Jack or Jill of all trades and the master/mistress of none," for the truth remains that ministers must be proficient and ripening in the various commissions. We don't have the luxury— whether in parish, education, or community-based ministries—of gravitating only to chosen areas of pressing interest.

In the chapters ahead I will be exploring the classic categories of ministry, because they have served us well throughout the centuries and still carry spiritual import. The ones I have selected, in no particular rank, are: **pilgrim, philosopher, proclaimer, pastor, prophet, priest, politician, and person.** I have abandoned some conventional ones such as prelate and padre, while folding others such as educator and evangelist within given commissions. In keeping with my proclivity to alliteration I was tempted to use the positive charges of poet, provocateur, peacemaker and pioneer, as well as the shadow categories of philanderer, phony, profiteer, prude, pushover, and pedant. There are plenty of other worthy ministerial titles such as comforter, crusader, visionary, and mystic. I have simply decided to revisit the proven commissions that comprise the parson's pathway.

I will emphasize service within the parish ministry since that is the domain I know best from personal experience, but it has become increasingly clear that my designated commissions are intricately interwoven in the work of community-based and educational ministries as well. I harbor no bias that any form or locale of professional ministry is superior to any other. After all, Mohammed and Mary Baker Eddy, Confucius and Mother Teresa, as well as most religious pioneers spread throughout the living tradition of ministry, hardly fit the resume of the conventional pastorate.

Additionally, it should be noted that the eight commissions I have chosen, although distinctive, are overlapping in practice. Ministers may prove particularly passionate about and proficient in one or two domains, even pick a specialized form of ministry such as chaplaincy or social service, teaching or counseling, but in the long run, we must display sufficient skill in all the commissions or our given ministry will suffer.

For example, ministers, wherever we serve, must be ambidextrous. We must be agile as both "strokers and rufflers," to use Martin Marty's evocative terms: "To omit the stroking is to deprive people of security. To neglect the ruffling is to give them divine sanctions for being content with themselves as they are and the world as it is." James Luther Adams refers similarly to the priest as the stabilizer and the prophet as the shatterer, roles integral to both congregational and societal life. Ministers are beckoned to become whole people speaking to the whole person.

To complicate matters, even within single ministerial commissions, parsons are saddled with the interweaving, dual functions of both consoling and confronting, educating and stretching the horizons of congregants. Political commentator H. L. Mencken used to talk about "comforting the afflicted and afflicting the comfortable." Sounds suspiciously like ministry!

Finally, the interlinking combinations within ministry are countless. Pilgrims must be part politician; philosophers concede that knowledge is hollow unless embodied in action; preaching is only decisive when bolstered by dependable pastoring; and authentic personhood undergirds every facet of the entire profession.

One of the central challenges in ministry is maintaining equilibrium, balancing our various gifts and duties lest we grow lopsided. It is tempting to put the bulk of one's time into research for sermons, or counsel endlessly, or gain prominence through public service, while neglecting the other equally important tasks critical to a full-spirited, full-service ministry. As Emerson warns ministers: "We are riders forever falling off one side of the horse or the other."

Maintain poise. Stay balanced.

THE CHALLENGE

D ragons are mystical, powerful, emerging out of mystery, disappearing in mystery, fierce, benign, known to teach humans the deepest reaches of wisdom. And dragons are filled with fire.

Brian Swimme

Medieval defenders had to slay their dragons; modern ones have to take their dragons back home to integrate into their own personality.

Robert Johnson

Never laugh at live dragons.

J. R. R. Tolkien

27

THE NATURE OF THE BEAST

Ministers in Western culture have grown up thinking in terms of right and wrong, good and evil, the angelic and the demonic, God and the Devil. It takes but a short while in actual ministry to acknowledge that matters are a thousand times more complicated. We are inevitably confronted not with a monolithic Devil so much as dragons: paradoxical beasts, immensely alluring and repulsive. As a classically power-driven profession, ministers have been trained to try, before entertaining other options, to conquer the dragons, a la St. George. But most seasoned parsons would vouch for the fact that ministry resembles the art of learning how to make peace with, not destroy, to shake hands with, not slay, the dragons.

Among the oldest of mythological creatures, dragons appear in numerous forms in the traditions of virtually all peoples back to the beginnings of time. In earliest cast, they were associated with the Great Mother, the water-god, and the warrior sun-god, and in these mixed capacities dragons embodied immense power to be both beneficent and destructive creatures in the universe.

Yet in Western mythology it is difficult to find a kind word about the dragon. One of the rare exceptions is the fairy tale *The Reluctant Dragon* by Kenneth Grahame, that tells of a dragon not wishing to fight the knight at all. We who grew up in Western civilization clearly are obsessed with the dragon as evil. There is an eternal enmity between reptiles and humans. Clergy prepare to be dragonslayers.

In Eastern lore dragons are wise and noble animals who were guardians of the Buddha and companioned kings. The emperor's royal seat in China was referred to as the Dragon's Throne and his countenance, the Dragon's Face. At the emperor's death it was said that he ascended to heaven like the dragon.

In Chinese mythology the dragon-horse is a messenger of

heaven who "revealed" Yin and Yang, the two faces of the universe, to the Yellow Emperor. Also, in the *I Ching*, the dragon symbolizes Wisdom. It appears as one of the four great constellations in Chinese astronomy, and the New Year is celebrated on the appearance of the moon before the rising of the dragon-star.

Consequently, dragons are the fitting mythological beast to describe the frightful enticements of ministry, since they are subtler than either the Devil, the formidable ruler of hell, or demons, purely evil spirits. We have joined a profession that is filled with baneful yet salutary challenges, with perilous yet dazzling promise, just like the dragon.

The Hindus espouse a shrewder understanding of the nature of good and evil than Western religions that drift toward absolute dichotomies. Hinduism recognizes that nothing is all good or all evil; everything in existence is a mixture of both. Hence, they celebrate their primary Fall festival, Divali, precisely on the birthday of an evil demon, Narakarasura, who was by no means all bad. It is difficult to imagine Western religionists featuring a holy-day in memory of Lucifer!

A comparable example is the contrast between our attitudes toward nature. When Westerners scale Mt. Everest they refer to the trek as the "conquest of Everest," while Asian climbers speak of "befriending Everest."

Pagan essayist Starhawk conveys a similar point in her book, *Dreaming the Dark*:

> *Our culture teaches men to deny fear and women to let fear control them. Yet if we learn to feel our fear without letting it stop us, fear can become an ally, a sign to tell us that something we have encountered can be transformed. Often our true strength is not in the things that represent what is familiar, comfortable, positive—but in our fears and even in our resistance to change.*

Ministry is about paying homage to the untamed powers of the unconscious as well as the primitive denizens of the outer sphere, for dragons live in both realms. Dragons cannot be denied; however, they can be faced, and, in most cases, befriended.

In addition to choosing dragons to symbolize the consummate challenge for ministry precisely because of their ambiguous nature, I confess to being attracted to dragons because of their picturesque, colorful quality. I have a whimsical, dazzling, slightly intimidating Mexican dragon on my desktop at work to remind me of the harrowing professional voyage I navigate daily.

Although largely pink and marked by a winsome smirk, my hand-crafted dragon also breathes fire. This wooden sculpture is a vivid reminder that dragons dwell in ocean depths, neither of our creation nor of our fathoming and, while living in water, they spew an intense blaze as fire-eating and breathing creatures. But fire cleanses and heals even as it sears and destroys. I often soften and suppress the fire in my own internalized dragon, lest it singe someone, when my ministry would be healthier and more effective if I dared to become a fierce, heated presence that burns brightly and bravely into the fabric of existence.

MINISTERIAL DRAGONS

This office is like being committed to wild beasts. What are these wild beasts? Wrath, dejection, envy, contention, slanders, accusations, falsehoods, hypocrisy, plots, ill-will toward such as have done no wrong, pleasure in the indecorous acts of one's fellow ministers, sorrow over their successes, love of praises, lust of honor, sordid flatteries, contempt for the poor, servile fear...

St. John of Chrysostom

There are plenty of mighty dragons cruising the oceans of our vocation, as attested to by the ominous listing of the medieval Christian St. John of Chrysostom. The seven deadly sins wreak havoc in ministry as well, but the most bewitching dragonish representative might just be what St. John called "servile fear."

I have chosen to explicate the anxieties and dreads of ministry because fear, like dragons, is attractive yet loathsome. In the conduct of ministry we are often drawn to and entangled with exactly that which revolts us.

Whereas the huge, awful dragons of plagiarism, lying, extortion, sexual misconduct, burnout, professional jealousy, and desertion have over the years wrought considerable damage in our profession, I would contend that it is the sneakier, less imposing dragons that cause ministers the steadiest grief. Much has been written about our sensational ministerial malaises and abuses, but little has been mentioned about the insidious fears that harry ministers on a daily basis. Richard Gilbert put it adroitly upon receiving a Doctor of Sacred Theology:

> *This award reminds me of a certain Lutheran Seminary which in its catalogue listed a degree of Master of Scared Theology. I have been trying to juggle these two letters, "a" and "c" for almost a quarter century now, and it is time I got it right. If the truth be known, the parish ministry is characterized as much by 'running scared' as 'mediating the sacred.'*

In addition to those ministerial dragons I enumerated earlier in my ministerial odyssey, let me catalogue some general ones now, with others to appear in later chapters. Most ministerial fears are not tied to one particular commission but cunningly interfuse the entire web of our profession. I have entered and conducted my ministry lugging my own peculiar bag of fears, but the following ones seem to carry common coinage in our vocation.

—Fear of being an impostor, so if parishioners really learned how little I know or believe, they might fire me on the spot.

—Fear of laughing uncontrollably during a rite-of-passage, ranting or railing in the pulpit, displaying blatant ignorance while teaching a newcomer's church history class, bungling a prayer at a community-wide event, revealing something "too personal" while counseling a parishioner.

—Fear of failing or falling flat—a dread that none of us ever quite relinquishes, but is exaggerated in ministry because of all our "chances" to do so publicly.

—Fear of retirement when we will no longer have access to a regular platform or predictable adulation.

—Fear of giving to our family leftovers of our energy and emotions after sacrificing ourselves at the church office.

—Fear of being damned falsely and having no viable recourse to rebut the slanderous rumors.

—Fear of being either too cowardly or too brazen in one's prophetic proclamations.

—Fear that in trying so hard to be all things to all "my church people," I will fail to be much of anything real or substantive to any of them.

—Fear that I will become so engulfed in human *doing* that I will lose touch with my human *being*.

—Fear that in a profession committed to cultivating the *spiritual*, I have little right to seek *material* comfort, or conversely, that laboring tirelessly every year on boosting the budget (including my own salary) vitiates any authentic effort to help members "grow their souls."

—Fear of being either too erudite or too pedantic as a religious educator.

—Fear of not quite knowing how to convey one's faith in language understandable to a child or youth.

—Fear of actually getting lost in the moral wilderness as a **pilgrim**.

—Fear of being so in love with abstract ideas as a **philosopher** that I grow out of touch with real people.

—Fear of running out of worthwhile things to say or having "my faith" as a **proclaimer** suddenly go stale or dry up.

—Fear of being a "sweetheart" as a **pastor**, trying to win everyone's approval but no one's respect.

—Fear of growing bored in doing rituals, losing the magic and mystery of **priestly** work.

—Fear of being caricatured as too sneaky, even machiavellian as a **politician**.

—Fear of becoming a radical rabble-rouser who is blind to conciliatory options as a **prophet**.

—Fear of succumbing to the malaise of "falling into the farmer" (Emerson), by trading my **personhood** in for a tantalizing bunch of roles.

Perhaps the consummate dragon underlying all the others is our ministerial fear of having labored for "naught" or being considered "insignificant" in the last analysis. We are notoriously "comparing" who we are and what we've done to see if we measure up with other clerics. As a result, we will do most anything to maintain worth in our own sight, as well as in the eyes of congregants, colleagues, and God.

A humorous tale that captures this pretentious need for self-promotion. There was a minister who early in his career served a midwestern river town. During a devastating deluge in that region, known as the "Great Flood," the minister displayed enormous personal courage, saving the lives of several people both within and outside his own home parish.

For the remainder of his life, as we ministers are wont to do, this parson regaled everyone he met with his heroic story. After dying, he arrived in Heaven and was greeted at the pearly gates by St. Peter, who forthwith invited him to introduce himself that evening to the Heavenly throng by making a few personal remarks.

"Oh, wonderful, great! I can tell everybody about my work during the Great Flood back in my beginning years as a minister!"

Peter was a bit taken back by the cleric's bursting pride, but he concurred: "Okay, that will be fine; go ahead and tell your glowing story of personal bravery during the midwestern Great Flood, but I must remind you that **Brother Noah** will be the audience tonight!"

So it goes.

The hopeful reality is that none of our ministerial dragons, however tenacious or imposing, furnishes an impossible challenge. In truth, within each peril resides a resourceful promise.

SHAKING HANDS WITH THE DRAGONS

To snap a wooden idol in two is extremely easy; but to break a dragon is a task beyond our power.

Rumi

Liberal ministers hardly acknowledge the tenacity, let alone the ineradicability of evil, while conservative clergy are hell-bent on cleansing the world of demons. In either scenario, ministers posit that their holy work can be sustained only if we are nice or tough enough, but the truth is that the dragons of existence are intractable realities that must be encountered face-to-face, ongoingly.

There are certainly moments in ministry when we must avoid, inveigle, or demolish dragons, but the healthiest posture is one of learning how to embrace the dragons—what the Chinese call shake hands with the dragons.

One of the songs of my seminary era (1963), "Puff the Magic Dragon," was rife with equivocal references to both delight and drugs while fableizing the need of the little child (Jackie Paper) in each of us to maintain a mutually nurturing bond with the magic dragons of our lives. "Without his lifelong friend, Puff could not be brave, so Puff that mighty dragon sadly slipped into his cave." Likewise, we ministers can easily slip into cavernous holes, whenever we fail to playfully companion the dragons of existence.

During the celebration of the Chinese New Year, people come up to the dragon and shake hands with it. As San Diegan Carl Glick muses in his 1941 volume *Shake Hands With the Dragon*:

> *If the dragon is nature in all her terror and majesty, let us not be afraid. Let us go out and meet that fear. It is only the unknown that frightens us. We cling to our hearthstones because we are afraid of what lies beyond that hill over there. But once we go out and explore that unknown country, our fear of it vanishes. Shake hands with the dragon, that's the way of Tao, the way of peace...to shake hands with the dragon.*

During the celebration of the Chinese New Year in San Francisco, young children walk inside an enormous paper dragon in a parade. People come up to the dragon and give it money, to bring good luck in the New Year, or "shake hands" with it, to muster courage for what the fresh slate of 365 days will bring. What a serviceable metaphor for satisfying and fulfilling ministry, for clergy and laity alike!

MINISTER AS PILGRIM

SAUNTERERS ON A SACRED JOURNEY

G o from your country and your kindred to the land that I will show you...I will bless you so that you will be a blessing.

Genesis 12:1-2

Search we must. Each one must set out to cross the bridge. The important thing is to begin. But, remember, setting out does not by itself guarantee success. There is beginning, but there is also persevering, that is, beginning again and again and again. You are well advised to set out with a professional pilgrim as a guide. And remember, too, you can stay at home, safe in the familiar illusion of certainty. Do not set out without realizing that 'the way is not without danger. Everything good is costly, and the development of the personality is one of the most costly of all things.' It will cost you your innocence, your illusions, your certainty.

Sheldon Kopp

39

No one's faith journey begins at birth. It starts eons back with the mothers and fathers of our great-grandmothers and great-grandfathers, and before. Our faith seeps into our corpuscles carried on the songs we hear before we know what their words mean...It comes to us bound up with caste and class, with color and gender, with language and cuisine. We all meet ourselves, as Soren Kierkegaard once put it, 'on a ship already launched, a journey already underway.'

Harvey Cox

Heroes/heroines take journeys, confront dragons, and discover the treasure of their true selves...Their task then is to bridge, not to slay or convert.

Carol Pearson

Come, come, whoever you are, wanderer, worshiper, lover of leaving. Ours is no caravan of despair. Come, yet again come.

Rumi (adapted)

One of the fundamental commissions of the ministry is being a pilgrim, a member of the unbroken human caravan, one who journeys in familiar lands and foreign seas as a wayfarer, trekking to shrines and holy places, as well as locating the sacred right where one resides. Revolutionary pilgrims aren't always on the move. They are both wanderers and dwellers, a people of the way and a people with an address. They may risk countless, bold shifts while remaining committed to the same partner and incarnate radically different versions of ministry while staying in the same profession, even village.

The pilgrim is a *saunterer*, literally a "holy-lander" who treats every step and piece of turf as a conveyor of holiness. They search, not merely *for*, but *with*, their very own stories and struggles, remaining a ready resource for other travelers along the journey. Pilgrims, despite the dull stretches and dry spells, are characterized as persistent plodders. They progress, they seek the next horizon.

As pilgrim, the minister has core duties as well as concomitant dragons to be encountered.

(I) Striding Inwardly and Outwardly

> *Keep your eye on the functioning of your inner life and start from there—to read, to pray, or to do any needed outward deed. If, however, the outward life interferes with the inner, then follow the inner; but if the two can go on together, that is best of all, and then we are working together with God.*
>
> Meister Eckhart

Pilgrimages are conventionally described as external trips, but ministers move physically from task to task, place to place, *and* continue growing internally as well. In fact, according to Eckhart, if any emphasis must be made, it should be upon exploration of one's inner trek. Our ministries are synchronized with the divine when there is a balance of inner and outer journeying.

(2) Wandering Alone and Accompanied

Ministry is indubitably a solitary excursion. Too few clergy grow a satisfying acquaintance with our own souls, since we are constantly wrapped up in interpersonal communion. Joseph Campbell was fond of quoting the passage from the legend of the Holy Grail where the Knights of the Round Table set forth on their quest:

> Each one went into the woods in the place where it was darkest and there was no path, for they thought it would be a shame to go in a group.

Yet ministry is a profession rotating both solitariness and solidarity. If we are stuck in our solitude we will become lonely, disconnected souls. Out of refulgent quietude, clergy bring resources to the communal journey we share with fellow travelers. It is essential to healthy ministry to maintain equilibrium between the two poles of existence, moving agilely back and forth between being apart and sharing kinship.

(3) Ambling Purposefully

Ministry is holy whenever it is purposeful. As religious forebear Ralph Waldo Emerson put it: "The purpose of life is not to be happy. It is to be useful, to be honorable, to be compassionate, to have it make some difference that you have lived and lived well." The soles of our feet must advance in service of the souls of our beings. Our vocation is holy not because we journey hither and yon, but when we travel toward our human destination: namely, restoring justice to the

42

commonweal and stewarding the earth's resources.

At some juncture in our vocational odyssey, clergy awaken to realize that humans have been placed on earth primarily to become meaning-makers. Who we are may be God's gift to us, but who we choose to become is our gift back to the universe. We can never repay the Creation for bringing us to life and showering us with bountiful blessings. We don't even need to try. Right livelihood resides in our leading human lives bountiful in gratitude that converts into compassion.

Pilgrims in the 4th and 5th centuries would travel to remote hermitages of the Desert Fathers and open a ritual exchange with the sentence: "Give me a word, that I may live!" On the various main roads and by-ways of the human pilgrimage, ministers are called upon to deliver saving words. Our purpose is clear and unified. Ministry is unreservedly dedicated to delivering hopeful, liberating, life-affirming news to all sisters and brothers who cross our pathway. "Good tidings," as Isaiah phrases it.

But dragons would entice us to confuse discipline with compulsion, purposefulness with domination. Pilgrim-ministers need to be in charge of our journeys without overmapping them. Undue control is what a guard does to a prisoner. Control will turn joyful commitments into tedious obligations.

(4) Being Visionaries

We are neither left nor right but in front, visionary.
European Greens

While traveling about, ministers aspire to amble a la Leonardo da Vinci, who moved about with a small sketchpad strapped to his belt, observing reality incessantly. Ministers require the vision of both *eagles* who view the overall landscape from afar and *mice* who experience details at ground level. Pilgrim-ministers harbor hunches about where beauty and justice lie, and, more importantly, have the courage to travel there, and coax, even goad, others to join the caravan.

Visionaries enable others to perceive and embody hope, what might yet become. We yank one another out of ruts, spring one another beyond mediocrity, exhort cohorts toward worthy destinations. Pilgrims gladden one another when vision is flagging and imagination is faint. Emerson once wrote:

> *Faith and love are apt to be spasmodic in the best minds. We live on the brink of mysteries and harmonies into which we never enter, and with our hands on the door-latch, we die outside.*

Visionaries urge people to take the risk and open life's doors. Clergy refuse to allow congregants to settle into the trap of being a religious community known as the "almost" people. We almost touched beauty. We almost loved. Religious folks are a people who choose to live not on the brink but in the very midst of mysteries and harmonies. Ministers exist to remind us of that vision, that possibility, that ideal, that charge.

(5) Zig-Zagging

> *Of true places, they are never down on any map.*
> Herman Melville

Pilgrims know, as my minister-wife puts it, how to step off the sidewalk, take detours, move circuitously through life. Although pursuing a certain goal, they remain willing and able to venture alternate routes. Pilgrims know that spiritual growth entails negotiating zig-zags because, as mythology has it, the Devil, who can only travel in a straight line, will then be left behind.

What kind of story are we religious travelers in? Is it a story of an adventure, a journey, a voyage of discovery? Yes, but at times it is something simpler, like the story of a child playing by the sea. "I do not know what I may appear to the world," Isaac Newton said in his old age, "but to myself I seem to have been only like a child playing on the seashore, and diverting myself in, now and then, finding a smoother pebble or a prettier shell than ordinary, whilst the great ocean of truth lay all undiscovered before me."

The Zen monk Ryokan lived as a hermit. According to his poems, Ryokan spent his life going down to the village and playing with the children during the day and then going way back in the woods to be by himself.

(6) Undertaking a Strenuous Journey

Nothing is secure, but life, transition and energizing spirit.
Ralph Waldo Emerson

*The root of travel is **travail**.*
William Matthews

We live in a pop-culture where intellectual and spiritual pabulum are dispensed daily, and directions for nirvana are passed out on street corners. But genuine religion has nothing to do with a pain-free, undemanding entrance into enlightenment. The way of Wandering Arameans, of pilgrims on an Exodus, is a lifelong quest, replete with dull stretches, harsh of body and soul, not for the fainthearted. Indeed, hardy pilgrims don't eschew difficulty, they entertain it. Alongside the hunter in Robert Bly's *Iron John*, they cry out: "Is there anything dangerous to do around here?" Pilgrims know you can get lost in life's barren deserts and ensnared in life's dense forests. They acknowledge that "easy" and "safe" are not terms to describe either religion or ministry.

Pilgrim-ministers enlist one and all in singing that noted Negro Spiritual:

Jesus walked this lonesome valley. He had to walk it by himself. Oh, nobody else could walk it for him. He had to walk it by himself.

Jesus isn't alone in walking the lonesome valley. The hymn continues by inviting the rest of us to join the arduous pilgrimage: "We must walk this lonesome valley by ourselves," then "we must go and stand our trial by ourselves" as well.

Upon revisiting the story of the American Pilgrims, one discovers additional lessons relevant to the strenuousness of shared ministry.

It is tempting to romanticize the story, the setting, the characters, and the virtues of the first Thanksgiving since, among other reasons, we are fearful of sullying our American image with the muddied reality. On the contrary, I find that I am more instructed, even inspired, upon realizing that the Pilgrims were as beastly and brave as humans of every era. It is consoling to know that they were more like us than not.

The Pilgrims comprised a motley handful of families who defied good sense in seeking to settle a wilderness in winter and to plant seeds of democracy in the new world. They came to build a way of life and a community that would be, as John Winthrop said, "a light unto the nations," a phrase directly echoing Jesus' great commission.

The challenge was more difficult than anyone could have imagined. In that first winter at Plymouth, over half of them died of starvation and exposure, including many children. The Pilgrims had to wonder whether the trek was really worth it after such devastation. Yet, wrote William Bradford in his modest journal: "They knew that they were pilgrims, and they summoned **answerable courages!**" Their courages, and Bradford rightly speaks in the plural here, were not of a supernatural kind but of earthly proportion. They summoned, from the depth of their beings, soul-sized courages.

We too are pilgrims, and a central ministerial charge is to remind religious people of that common role. In our modern epoch of hardship and tumult, different difficulties to be sure, we are constantly pressed into summoning "answerable courages." If Bradford had talked about the courages of the Pilgrims as being glorious and awesome, then most people would continue to perceive them in godly rather than human terms. "Answerable" means possible, it means responsible, it means the Pilgrims did what they had to do to survive the winter and settle the new land.

Another forgotten twist of the first Thanksgiving humanizes the situation even further. The Pilgrims came to America because of ingratitude. They were dissatisfied with the conditions of life in their homeland. They reflected Martin Luther King, Jr.'s attitude of "creative maladjustment." Such discontent signals the human spirit breaking out of prison houses of the past toward newer and more resourceful worlds. If the Pilgrims had only been a smug, self-satisfied lot, they would have never left home in the first place. The role of ingratitude in our lives ought never be underestimated.

The Pilgrims began in disgruntlement yet ended in thanksgiving. This bruised and beaten-down crew of travelers, instead of blaming God for their travail, got down on their knees and sang the Creator's praises.

As twentieth-century religious saunterers we are indebted to human forebears such as the Pilgrims and innumerable others, in world history and in our own personal stories, upon whose shoulders we now stand. The book of Deuteronomy issues a stark reminder: "You drink here from cisterns that you did not dig and you live in cities that you did not build and you eat from vineyards and orchards that you did not plant." Indeed we do. Our religious response is to exude gratitude and compassion, while passing on soulful riches and resources to those around us and those coming after us.

(7) Surviving with Passionate Equanimity

> *I detect in you, Loran, a good head for Talmud. But you have no enthusiasm. You are without **entheos**. You are without the feeling of possession by the divine. There is no fire burning in you.*
>
> Chaim Potok

Enthusiasts (literally, the "god-filled") are those ministers who exude passionate devotion to the marvels of life, carry a burning fire in their hearts, more than a mere spark. Yet beware, for the necessary posture in ministry is to be ablaze with spirit without being consumed. Therein skulks another dragon.

In the poignant story of Treya Wilber's battle with cancer, retold by her husband Ken Wilber in the book *With Grit and Grace*, Treya centers, in her closing months, upon a phrase that captures the heart of her soulful struggle with living-and-dying, and aptly summarizes the core of ministerial endeavor: "passionate equanimity."

As pilgrim-ministers we travel with zestfulness, not nonchalance. Deep sentiments such as sorrow, love, and joy are outgrowths of a fervent soul. Passion fuels our compassion as well. Augustine spoke once of the "love which awakens love's response." There is nothing deadlier than a pious yet passionless pilgrimage in the ministry. No renewal will occur within our congregations until there is a recovery of passion among our religious professionals. In the name of being fair-minded and appropriately detached, ministers can dragonize into frozen, juiceless leaders.

Joanna Macy reminds us that working with purpose entails three conjoined ingredients: working with our passion, working with our pain, and working with what is directly at hand. Working not with somebody else's passion or pain but our very own. Each of us, if we but draw deeply upon it, contains a wellspring of passion. If truth be told, passion can be easily lost somewhere between an evening meeting of the Finance Committee and dealing with a bullheaded church member. Passion is not easy to sustain. Parsons regularly fall in and out of love with the ministry rather than developing gradual delight in our profession.

If one dragon confronts ministers via our reluctance to exuberance, another greets us when we mistake debilitating compulsions for healthy passions. There is a fine line in my own ministry between being in the driver's seat and being driven, between being a productive person and one stuck on results, between governing my own existence and trying to run the lives of those around me. I traverse that tightrope, sometimes agilely and sometimes shakily.

The key distinction to remember is that whereas my *passions* should enhance congregational life, ministerial *addictions* will inevitably drain or diminish it.

(8) Traveling Leanly and Lightheartedly

> *One definition of sin and idolatry is being weighed down with so much luggage we lose the purpose of the trip. David went against Goliath leanly prepared. He did not accept the proffered armor. It would have been his death. And the saints? They travel light. That way they can look and see and relate and heal. That way they can hear the music and dance.*
>
> Clarke Wells

Lest the religious journey become unduly rugged and grim, it must be undertaken with a buoyant heart. True pilgrims travel with a light spirit and few belongings. They embrace living, then dying, and therewith join Antonio Machado in his magnificent poetic invitation:

> *And when the day arrives for the last leaving of all,*
> *And the ship that never returns to port is ready to go,*

You'll find me on board, light, with few belongings,
Almost naked like the children of the sea.

I am fond of the story where in the last century, a tourist from the States visited the famous Polish Rabbi Hafez Hayyim. He was astonished to see that the rabbi's home was only a simple room filled with books. The only furniture was a table and bench. "Rabbi, where is your furniture?" asked the tourist. "Where is yours?" replied Hafez. "Mine? But I'm only a visitor here." "So am I," said the rabbi.

We are all short-timers on this earthly plane. Such consciousness mandates that we choose carefully what we will own, how we will arrange our primary dwellings, and how we will steward—neither exploit nor merely manage—the resources with which we have been blessed. Pilgrims take their earthly trip purposefully yet playfully.

In terms of ministry, this means that every one of our posts, whether lasting one year or twenty-five years, has a specific beginning and end. As Rosemary Smurzynski puts it baldly: "You are my people and I am your minister, for a while!" Every ministry is an interim one and to be treated as such. We ministers are not church owners but shareholders along with the laity.

Ministry ultimately resembles life: We end our time or tenure somewhere in the middle with yet more tasks and dreams ahead of us, with certain things finished and others yet to be realized.

(9) Roaming As Trustful Agnostics

Sam Keen makes a useful distinction between a religious pilgrimage and a spiritual quest:

The former is to a known destination. The end is given as
well as the means. God is the goal of the search. Church, bible,

guru, and the accepted disciplines of the spirit are the means. You are treading where the saints have trod. The latter begins when an individual falls into a spiritual 'black hole' in which everything that was solid vaporizes. Certainties vanish, authorities are questioned, all the usual comforts and assurances of religion fail, and the path disappears.

A skillful minister is one who assists fellow congregants in managing both religious pilgrimages and spiritual quests. Neither is preferable to the other. There is a place and time for each, and the sensitive pilgrim-minister knows how to conduct both journeys.

However, since ministers are sometimes perceived to be messengers of certitude, it is sobering to remember that we are actually pilgrims dwelling in an atmosphere of "trustful agnosticism" (Keen's phrase). Amidst creative uncertainty, it is calming to my soul to sing every morning during spiritual discipline time the following lighthearted chant: "I am moving on a journey to nowhere, taking it easy, taking it slow, no more hurry, no more worry, nothing to carry, let it all go!"

To see one's life as a journey, as a ceaseless adventure or discovery, as an opportunity to learn from one's joys and sorrows furnishes an insightful perspective. But let's not get carried away. Many of us can identify with the Zen story that satirizes the concept of the holy pilgrimage. The guru rests on his deathbed and gasps his last words to his assembled followers: "Life is a Journey." As this closing profundity is passed around in hushed whispers, the newest of his disciples loudly and irreverently challenges this assertion. The guru himself hears this, reconsiders, and so the absolutely last words his disciples hear are: "So, life is not a Journey?"

Journey or not, we are all in this together.

MINISTER AS PHILOSOPHER

SEEKERS AND SHARERS OF WISDOM

There are few human beings, who, when they think of themselves in relation to the universe, are without a sense of curiosity, of wonder, and even of awe; and insofar as this leads them into speculation, they become philosophers.

L. H. Myers

No one is my master. Anyone may be my teacher.

Zen Buddhism

I am grateful for the Idea that has used me.

Felix Adler

'A philosopher,' said the theologian, 'is like a blind person in a darkened room looking for a black cat that isn't there.' 'That's right,' the philosopher replied, 'and if one were a theologian, they would find it!'

Anonymous

If your philosophy breaks down and you can fix it yourself, they should make you a doctor of philosophy.

Philip Berman

*For **Sophia** is more beautiful than the sun,
and excels every constellation of the stars.
Compared with the light she is found to be superior,
For it is succeeded by the night,
but against wisdom evil does not prevail.*

Wisdom of Solomon (7:29-30)

Minister-philosopher literally signals "one who loves wisdom," a questor who travels beyond infatuation with knowledge, magic, or the occult. Although there is clearly a place for theologians, "students of God," in ministry I have always considered philosopher to be the broader, more inclusive designation.

Philosophers are scholars in the richest senses: lifelong students as well as enjoyers of rest and ease (from the original Greek). Carl Sandburg spoke eloquently about the union of learning and leisure when he remarked about the Glassy Mountain near his home:

> I often walk here to be alone. Solitude is an essential part of a person's life and sometimes we must seek it out. I sit here and I look at the silent hills and I say, 'Who are you, Carl? Where are you going? What about yourself, Carl?'

Philosophers study, contemplate, calculate, reason, and intuit. They synthesize as well as analyze. They employ the strategies of the logician and those of the mystic. They are filled with both intellectual exuberance and spiritual wonder.

Ministry is about plumbing the depths of existence, then offering up one's learnings bathed in an atmosphere of astonishment.

In 1972, Jewish philosopher Abraham Heschel suffered a near-fatal heart attack from which he never fully recovered. When Heschel regained consciousness, his first feelings were not of despair or anger but of gratitude to God for his very existence—for every moment he had lived. He was ready to depart. "Take me, O Lord, I have seen so many miracles in my lifetime" were his words echoing what he wrote in the preface to his book of Yiddish poems: "I did not ask for *success*; I asked for *wonder*. And you gave it to me."

(I) Probing Life's Depths

> Search for nothing anymore, nothing except truth. Be very still, and try to get at the truth. And the first question to ask yourself is: 'How great a liar am I?'
>
> D. H. Lawrence

> The task of the novelist (minister) is to deepen mystery, but mystery is a great embarrassment to the modern mind.
>
> Flannery O'Connor

> The religious way is the deep way, the way with a growing perspective and an expanding view. The religious way is the way that sees what physical eyes alone fail to see, the intangibles at the heart of every phenomenon. The religious way is the way that touches universal relationships, that goes high, wide and deep, that expands the feelings of kinship...
>
> Sophia Fahs

> There is always an enormous temptation in all of life to diddle around making itsy-bitsy friends and meals and journeys for itsy-bitsy years on end. The world is wilder than that in all directions, more dangerous and bitter, more extravagant and bright. We are making hay when we should be making whoopee; we are raising tomatoes when we should be raising Cain, or Lazarus.
>
> Annie Dillard

Jesus' invitation to Peter to "drop the nets into the deep" (Luke 5:1-9) symbolizes a similar request given to all ministers to dive below the surface and to perform our vocations with greater consciousness and meaning, living as the Psalmist exhorts: "deep calling unto deep."

Ministry is unmistakably a call to profundity and not away from it. None of us who answers the call to ministry dares resemble Captain McWhirr, whom Joseph Conrad describes in *Typhoon* as sailing "over the surface of oceans as some people go skimming through the years of existence to sink gently into a placid grave, ignorant of life to the last, without ever having seen all it may contain of perfidy, of violence and of terror." Dragons habitually intimidate parsons into paddling about in tidepools rather than plunging into the deeper waters of reality.

We ministers are tempted to play it safe, turn didactic or pedestrian, avoid venturing farther than six inches below the surface. To use a sea figure, some clergy seldom get "out of soundings." When a ship has beneath her keel more depth of water than can be plumbed by the lead line, the vessel is, in mariner's language, "out of soundings." Ministry that never gets "out of soundings" is not faithful stewardship of the intricate mysteries of God. There is an immeasurable profundity to the universe, and ministerial voyages must surge beyond the shallows to fathom vast resources for life's far-flung needs.

Depth has everything to do with sorrow and grief as well as joy and creativity. Ecclesiastes 2:18 offers: "For in much wisdom is much grief, and they who increase their knowledge increase their sorrow." If we would be wise, our spirits must remain open to wider sorrow and deeper grieving. Dragons often lure clergy away from paying the full price of wisdom.

(2) Entertaining a Wide Horizon

Ministry is not only a deep place but also a wide calling. "All my friends advised against the ministry," wrote Theodore Parker, one of the stellar 19th century minister-philosophers in America. "They said it was a narrow place, affording no opportunity to do much!" On the contrary, Parker deemed ministry "a wide place." And so it is, as expansive as existence itself.

Philosopher-ministers encourage innumerable pathways to the Supreme within our own souls as well as those of our fellow wisdom-seekers. As the New Testament offers: "Wisdom is justified by all her children..." (Luke 7:35), denoting that faith-communities hold varieties of religious experience within their fold.

Some questors will arrive at their vision of the holy primarily through reasoned faith, others through empirical observations or intuitive epiphanies, still others through compassionate action. As ministers we are commissioned to support all sacred routes that are honorably held and respectful of others. As Jesus phrased it: "In my Father's house are many rooms..." (John 14:02), not one sanctioned chamber alone, and the word for "salvation" in the Old Testament connotes a broad and spacious place. Truly saving wisdom will free the whole of creation **from** hindering conditions while liberating one and all **for** enlivening existence.

Philosopher-ministers refuse to make premature peace with our ignorance but keep bursting narrow conceptions and prejudicial comforts. We are serendipitous rather than systematic thinkers, seizing bits of truth from hither and yon, while steadily advancing through life's entanglements and ecstasies. Clergy assist congregations in joining the eternal quest for increasing wisdom, not merely greater erudition or subtler technique. Hence, our beloved communities must be intentionally diverse and welcoming to the panoply of classes, colors, capabilities, and convictions. It is our function as ministers to be multi-lingual with respect to variant religious philosophies—to manifest our own theological preferences while simultaneously undergirding others navigating their own routes toward divine wisdom.

(3) Educating

> *The great end in religious instruction is not to stamp our minds upon the young, but to stir up their own: not to impose religion upon them in the form of arbitrary rules, but to awaken the conscience, the moral discernment. In a word, the great end is to awaken the soul.*
>
> William Ellery Channing

> *Or what person is there among you, who, if your children ask for bread, will give them stones?*
>
> Matthew 7: 9

True philosopher-ministers are educators or what my friend calls "rabbinisters." Clergy garner considerable savvy and a cumulative body of knowledge in a range of diverse fields during seminary training, but it is arrogant to assume *mastery* before, during, or after theological education. As wise as we aspire to be, we never quite earn the degree of Master of Theology. Dragons furtively tempt ministers to presume the lofty status of master theologians when we belong to the priesthood of all believers where every woman and man holds equal access to the same information and kinship with the Holy. Ministers all too gladly seize, or are granted by unwitting laity, the status of "brighter or holier than thou."

Whatever knowledge or expertise clergy garner, it is to be shared for edification of the entire congregation rather than hoarded for personal aggrandizement. Rabbinisters are held accountable for "drawing out" (literal meaning of *educare*) as well as transmitting the substance of our religious heritage, thus building a community wherein both pulpit and pew are deemed teacher-learners.

Over two hundred years ago, religious pioneer John Wesley was impelled to remind his colleagues of their responsibility: "Wherever there are ten children in a Society, spend at least one hour with them twice a week. And do this, not in a dull, formal manner, but in earnest, with your might...Do it, or else you are not called to be a Methodist preacher. Do it as you can, till you can do as you would."

It remains our institutional responsibility as philosophers to be active, intimate educators in the lives of the younger members of our congregation. This provides a challenging commission, since many parish ministers are frightened of relating to children and youth, let alone teaching them regularly every week. Clergy are inclined either to ignore that zone of church life or to delegate it to others, but minister-philosophers are truly religious educators and are not given the option of relinquishing that responsibility.

(4) Co-Creating a Core Curriculum

Religious education constitutes a curriculum from which we never graduate. The concept of curriculum literally refers to the "course" for a foot race traditionally held in the great ancient amphitheaters. In religious education we occasion few athletic competitions (other than perhaps relay races at picnics), but rather introduce courses that focus upon those meanings integral to growing one's soul. The very process of determining what is central, secondary, or irrelevant to a core religious curriculum is a valuable endeavor cooperatively shaped by clergy and laity, young and old alike.

—The curriculum comprises a body of wisdom balanced between personal enrichment, social justice, and spiritual growth.

—The curriculum generates program materials that substantiate the shared gospel of one's common tradition, exploring the same central themes in age-appropriate ways.

—The curriculum should be neither child-centered nor adult-centered but congregation-centered, focused not upon mastering books but on fashioning religious community.

—The curriculum will draw primarily upon the resources of its singular staff and laity but occasionally, when desirable, will include specialized gifts of teachers from the greater society in which we live, being cautious not to duplicate what is done better or equally well elsewhere.

—The curriculum needs to include various and sundry retreats where the entire community plays, worships, serves, and communes together away from the homesite.

—The curriculum requires ministers to be imaginative and fresh programmers who resonate with Rumi's poetic phrase: "Start a huge, foolish project, like Noah. It makes absolutely no difference what people think of you." Certain activities will be pruned or die a natural death each year, even as new programs are conceived.

Upon his deathbed, the Plato is reported to have told Socrates that "the purpose of human existence is to practice dying." Knowing how to say farewell to lost dreams and broken relationships, aging bodies and provincial viewpoints is fundamental to the religious curriculum.

(5) Forging an Intergenerational Community

Philosopher-ministers pursue wisdom from every living tradition, secular as well as sacred, then share their discoveries alongside everyone in their congregation. No one is exempt from endless religious growth and learning. What an irreparable loss, if we adults and children who inhabit the same church premises throughout the years never really spend adequate time in one another's company, remaining unfamiliar with what causes each other sheer joy and acute pain!

Authentic intergenerationality is not an issue of equal capabilities or accountability but of equal worth where the gifts and yearnings of all ages are uniformly valued. Children, youth, and adults grow to honor one another as different yet respectful allies in creating a community that is livelier, more expansive and wondrous than one any age group could conceivably create by itself.

Clearly, children and youth experience their religious home somewhat differently than we adults do. And well they should. Distinct ages, interests, and developmental needs abound. And yet, underneath our differences, similar hungers and hurts circulate both in the young and the old. Youth aren't the only ones negotiating the highwire act between freedom and responsibility. Children aren't the only ones exploding with wonder and imagination. And adults aren't the only ones aware of our shortcomings, needing to repair relationships, anxious about mortality.

Children and youth come to their religious home to love and be loved. And so do the older folks. We adults arrive in order to grow an abiding sense of kinship with self, nature, neighbor, and divine reality. And so do our children. We are all troubled and seek to make meaning out of the seasons of sorrow. We all know what it feels like to be scared or awestruck, guilty or exhilarated. Intergenerational community offers the sacred chance to share our sentiments with fellow-travelers of ages other than our own, with spiritual buddies who are tied to us not by biological genes or social cause but by religious affinity.

Adult religion can become drab and predictable without the presence of the littler ones. In German the word for blessedness is *seelisch* and is etymologically related to our word "silly" reminding serious, sober adults that in order to be blessed we will have to become irrepressible practitioners of silliness, becoming not childish but childlike, thereby entering the realm of God.

When young people graduate from our religious education program and go off to work, school, or another village, we hold exit interviews, asking them one basic question: "What do you remember most fondly from your religious growth and learning experiences at First Church?" When pressed, they can articulate some of our stated principles, then specific peers and adults usually come into focus; but above all else they cherish the intergenerational revelry we enjoyed in shared company.

Our high school graduates talk glowingly about candlelight services and Martin Luther King, Jr. marches. They recall Saturday work projects where their contributions were esteemed by the elders of the tribe. They talk about the all-church parties, where everybody danced with everybody else, where various ages of our tribe had a jolly, uninhibited time, without chemical lubrication, luxuriating in what Sarah McCarthy calls "our own liberating ludicrousness and practicing being harmlessly deviant." They simply remember with stunning clarity and delight those moments when they-and-we were living out our grand mission as an intergenerational community.

In thinking back upon his life, Elie Wiesel noted how he had encountered, in the course of his spiritual wanderings, strange and inspiring teachers and fellow travelers who, each in her or his own way, gave Wiesel something for his journey: "a phrase, a wink, an enigma. And I was able to continue." Our children covet our phrases, our winks, our enigmas. We covet theirs. We need one another to be able to continue our respective pilgrimages.

MINISTER AS PROCLAIMER

DELIVERING HOPEFUL NEWS

Words are critical in shaping worlds. Lamentably, in modern culture "to preach" is associated pejoratively with dispensing moral advice in a tiresome manner. That need not be the case. Lively preaching can be both enlightening and inspirational, a goad for personal transformation and social change.

As Proverbs relates: "the tongue has power of life and death; make friends with it and enjoy its fruits." (18:21) Furthermore, whether one serves in a community, education, or parish-based ministry, clergy are ongoingly involved in the delivery of hopeful news through deeds and words. The contexts of ministry will vary, but the communication challenge remains constant.

(I) Claiming, then Disclosing, Our Gospel

The purity of heart is to will one thing.

Soren Kierkegaard

Sometimes people ask me how I keep thinking up new ideas for sermons. I don't. I have a few ideas that are fairly sound which I think I can vouch for, and I just keep using them again and again. Someone once said that politicians make the same speech as they move around to different audiences; and college professors make the same speech as the audiences move in front of them over the years; but preachers keep giving the same speech to the same people year after year. My hope is that eventually it will sink in.

Webster Kitchell

Every sermon should expound one cardinal truth. Ministers delivering, as well as laity hearing, should be able to describe the homily's central point in a single sentence. Indeed, every sermon is but a refined variation upon your principal

67

gospel. Ministers are frequently gripped by the malaise of *novophilia*—"loving the new simply because it's new."

Martin Buber, the greatest Jewish theologian of the twentieth-century, had a career of imposing complexity, yet his *I and Thou* concept permeated his entire work. "Reverence for life" did so for Albert Schweitzer. Mother Teresa has majored in unconditional compassion for God's marginalized ones. "Reconciliation" was foundational for Martin Luther King, Jr. My own version of the gospel would urge returning love to the Eternal Love that produced me, sustains and enfolds me forever, come what may. My responsive love is embodied through wholehearted immersion in and embrace of the Creation.

Preachers must proclaim their own particular version of redemptive news. We can never adequately preach the "good tidings" of another, whether we be orthodox Christians, Buddhists, or Moslems or whatever. Our personal idiosyncrasies of temperament and conviction must radiate in our proclamation. Both biblical testaments (Deuteronomy 6:4-5 and Mark 12:29-30) exhort us to "love the Lord Thy God with all thy heart, and with all thy soul, and with all thy might"—that is, not with someone else's being but with our own inimitable **thou-ness** and with the full measure of our singular devotion.

(2) Moving from Heart to Heart

> *A poem is never a put-up job. It begins as a lump in the throat, a sense of wrong, a homesickness, a lovesickness.*
> Robert Frost

> *Preach as you would speak to someone you love: not spectral, jargon language or public utterances.*
> Frederick Buechner

A sermon, like a poem, never starts or closes in abstractions. Good preaching evokes the stirrings of our souls as filtered through our minds. Unfortunately, some of our sermons are more like the miracle of Mohammed's coffin, suspended between heaven and earth, but actually touching neither. We preachers must avoid the fog of vague generalities. The place to start in the preparation and delivery of a sermon is the heart. The challenge is to employ personal illustrations rather than logical analysis, to be conversational rather than sociological. "Words that come from the heart enter the heart," says the Talmud, and as Proverbs 4:23 notes: "Out of the heart are the issues of life."

Clarity is related. Using big, fancy-sounding words often muddles communication. Civil-rights activist James Bevel used to warn: "The trouble with the average preacher is they speak about mendacity and prevarication and listeners still don't know whether or not the parson is against lying!" The purpose of preaching is, pure and simple, to reach the heart of the hearer.

An inspired misprint appeared in a newspaper story recording that the preacher's text was, "Though I speak with the tongues of humans and of angels and have not *clarity*, it profiteth me nothing."

(3) Creative Brooding

The greatest sins against communication are to speak when you're not moved and to fail to speak when you are.
Scott Peck

One day in the House of Commons, British Prime Minister Benjamin Disraeli made a brilliant speech on the spur of the moment. That night a friend said to him, "I must tell you how much I enjoyed your extemporaneous talk. It's been on my mind all day." "Madam," confessed Disraeli, "that extemporaneous talk has been on my mind for twenty years!"

The power of preaching resides primarily in the preparation: studious research, prayerful meditation, reflected life experience, dream scrutiny, and creative brooding, so that when we are ready to speak, we offer not necessarily a gem but a worthy and honorable gift.

Creative brooding can generate considerable anxiety. Ministers who claim to be void of anxiety may be disavowing the untamed edges of their inner souls. While anxiety can prove constructive and energizing, terror is inhibiting. If we clergy find ourselves caught in the clutches of debilitating panic while preaching, then we probably would benefit from outside counseling to pacify the rampaging dragons.

What brooding is to preparation, pausing is to delivery. Time must be allowed for those in the pew to preach to themselves. Sermons are a stimulating interplay of speaking and silence. A dragon appears in our ministries whenever we rush prematurely to fill a void or respite with words. "Rests" in music and "pauses" in preaching are imperative to create the richest communion.

When nervous or frustrated in our preaching, we are inclined to imitate Job:

> Job opens his mouth in empty talk. He multiplies words without knowledge. (Job 35:16)

Precisely when we think we're missing the mark in a sermon, we increase the volume or pile on words. We assume that just one more paragraph will turn the trick. We open our mouths in empty talk. I have been chided on more than one occasion when my address needlessly rambled on. Martin Luther used to say that every preacher needs to exercise "the power to leave off."

(4) Aiming High

Naturally there are topics that seize our attention and generate passion both in sermon research and elocution. But preachers know that we must "give our all" every Sunday rather than wait around to be "duly inspired." It is sensible to preach every sermon as if it were our last one, because someday it will be.

One of the supreme "preacher's fables" among the parables of Jesus is that of the friend at midnight, with its haunting confession of inner bankruptcy: "A friend of mine in his journey has come to me, and I have nothing to set before him." Every Sunday, parishioners, known and unknown, come to worship from journeys, both rough and disturbing, and covet a gospel of hope set before them. One of the most reinforcing affirmations I received early in my ministry came from a woman who said: "Tom, more often than not I happen to disagree with your viewpoint, but you usually deliver a message of promise and uplift. Your encouraging gospel keeps me coming back!" We clergy must aspire to speak not from cheery optimism but reasoned hopefulness.

Strangely enough, what doesn't move us parsons in our study may inspire listeners in the pew. Some of my finest sermons (or so I thought) reached few congregants, whereas homilies I wish hadn't left my lips were uncommonly transformative. The Holy Spirit moves in mysterious ways, but surely banks on our finest efforts every time we enter the pulpit.

A young apprentice once complained to Phillips Brooks, a notable American preacher, that nobody seemed to be affected by his attempts at preaching. Brooks responded, "You don't expect people to be changed every time you preach, do you?" The young man replied, "Why, of course not!" Brooks thundered at him. "That's your problem!"

(5) Being Vocal

When in doubt, read what you have written out loud. Computers lead to flabby and tone-deaf writing. We pay dearly for this convenience.

Garrison Keillor

My voice is my instrument. I cannot put it away in a case. It is not in the throat, from where it appears to come. It is in my feet and how they touch the floor, in my legs and how they lift and sink with the rhythm of the song. It is in my lungs, so strong and willing, and in my heart. My mouth and tongue and cheekbones are the sound box, the amplifier, the resonator, but they must resist the temptation to interfere. And when I am willing, all sound is available to me...and I find my voice.

Holly Near

Ministry is a vocation wherein the voice is paramount: we speak to invoke, evoke, provoke responses. There are ample opportunities in this chosen craft to be wordsmiths who compose taut, incisive essays to be read. I am not opposed to printed sermons, but let us never be fooled into equating them with the existential exchange that occurs between pulpit and pew. Preaching is meant to be heard. As such, it requires opening wide the larynx and projecting directly from the abdomen, not just from the teeth forward. Aikido, yoga, singing, and physical exercise all help preachers get in touch with the belly beneath our throats.

We need to find our voices (meaning both sound and message) as ministers, then methodically develop them into increasingly self-assured instruments of power. If as much time were expended in practicing one's oral delivery as in revising one's text, both preacher and congregant would be experiencing more dramatic, livelier sermons.

Minister-proclaimers are urged to speak out and speak forth, lest our wisdoms simply go unheard or unnoticed. One of the dragons I face in preaching remains my senseless fear that if I speak robustly from my deeper being, I might prove shrill, unleash personal anxieties, bowl people over. A strong voice need not be a strident one.

Preaching is more persuasive when pitch and intensity modulate: speaking loudly then gently, slowly then swiftly.

But, in every instance, what matters most is speaking to be heard, for a sermon that is not heard cannot be understood, let alone lived.

(6) Offering Difficult Truths Gently

I swear that I will never aspire to be a preacher of pretty sermons. I'll keep them rough just to escape the temptation of degenerating into an elocutionist.

Reinhold Niebhuhr

True speaking is not solely an expression of creative power; it is an act of resistance, a political gesture that challenges politics of domination, that would render us nameless and voiceless. As such it is a courageous act, as such it represents a threat.

bell hooks

If it's both true and painful, say it softly.

Larry Dunham

There are two invitations here. The first is to remember to be brave enough to preach more than convenient and agreeable sermons, succumbing to the dragon that would swallow us up in the tyranny of politeness. The purpose of a sermon is not to elicit love from congregants but to inspire soulful growth and incite moral action.

Sometimes parishioners will comment that they want to be challenged, even critiqued, by the minister's sermons, but seldom is that the case as regular fare. Bill Jacobsen claims that his congregation urged him "to raise some hell," since they considered his preaching too tame and sweet. "When I did," Jacobsen muses, "church members balked, saying: 'Hey, we meant for you to give *others* hell, not *us*!'"

The second reminder balances the first. When I know that I will be preaching a harsh message that may rub people raw, I preach it tenderly and may even dress more conservatively than usual to

73

minimize unnecessary communication roadblocks. Preaching style and substance remain in service of creative persuasion, for the consummate task of proclamation is communion rather than either performance or coercion. Just as the Holy Spirit lures ministers into compassionate service, so should preaching lure hearers into heeding the good and holy life.

(7) Dialoguing

> Dialogue, that is speech between people, is multi-vocal or many-voiced. When dialogue occurs, minds and heart and wills meet and many presences are felt. The moment of dialogue belongs to no one, yet it is the possession of all.
>
> Charles Bartow

Dialogical preaching seldom comes early in one's ministry. It takes years of being close to one's parishioners in times of crisis and joy, sharing projects and solving dilemmas, allowing abundant trust to ripen. There are Sundays when Carolyn and I, who have mutually served our San Diego congregation nearly 20 years, look out from the chancel toward the pews and review knowingly in the silence of our hearts the aches and struggles of our beloved partners in ministry. And parishioners view us in return, equally mindful of our agonies and ecstasies.

After so many years of enjoying a common pilgrimage and creating a mutual gospel, we are embedded within one another's very hearts and souls. It would be worshipful enough some Sundays just to sit wordlessly together, pulpit and pew, affirming our unspeakable bond with one another as the holy spirit meanders among us, then to conclude with a benediction of mutually bowing and speaking the simple Hindu blessing, *Namaste*: "the divine in my soul embraces the divine in yours!" We could then depart for home, without benefit of conversation or refreshments, yet amply buttressed for the week's trials and tribulations.

Specific tactics exist that enhance dialogue between pulpit and pew such as talkbacks, creating sermons together earlier in the week, speaking directly to the chosen topics of laity, doing conjoint sermons with congregants. Yet the mystery of mutuality can happen when one person speaks alone. It is born of reciprocal pastoring between pulpit and pew, what Adrienne Rich calls "a severer listening."

I remember my ego "puffing up" after a worship service when a visitor came through the "reception line" (there must be a better phrase to describe this awkward ritual) and said: "What a fine sermon today, Reverend!" Never knowing what one will hear in the "line," especially from newcomers, I quickly responded: "Why, thank you, thank you very much!" Then she responded: "No, I didn't mean the sermon you preached, but rather the one taking shape in my own heart while you were speaking!" Indeed, preaching remains a dialogical enterprise full of startling twists.

(8) Marching Orders

> The test of a preacher is that the congregation goes away saying not, 'What a lovely sermon, but, I will do something!'
>
> St. Francis de Sales

When Demosthenes, the famed Greek orator, first spoke in public, he was hissed off the platform. His voice was harsh and weak and his appearance unimpressive. He determined that his fellow citizens would yet appreciate his words, so he practiced day and night. He shaved half his head so no one would distract him with social events. To overcome a stammer, he recited with pebbles in his mouth and yelled against the thunders of the Aegean Sea, so his voice would get louder.

Demosthenes stood beneath a suspended sword to train himself not to favor a shoulder that kept hitching. He practiced facial expressions in front of a mirror. It's not surprising that when he next appeared in public, Demosthenes utterly moved the Greek nation. He and another orator spoke on a matter of national concern. When his companion concluded his speech, the crowd said, "What marvelous oratory!" But when Demosthenes finished, they cried with one voice, "Let's go and fight Philip!"

Now, few of us would employ such drastic measures to effect congregational response, but we could all learn from this ancient exemplar. He did what it took. Preaching is finally not about rhetoric but results.

(9) Interweaving Proclamation And Comfort

I have decided that ministry can be summed up in two words: **comfort** *and* **proclamation**, *and miraculously the two are one...When the New Testament speaks of the Holy Spirit as the Comforter, we know what it means, and when Paul speaks of "sin against the Holy Spirit," we know whereof he speaks. Comfort is the first and final calling of the minister. Yet more is commanded. We are to proclaim liberty, justice, warning, deliverance, faithfulness, praise, light, eternal life.*

David Parke

Good preaching and good pastoring are intertwined. Every sermon must bring sufficient comfort both in its delivery and content. The core of Isaiah's gospel is the proclamation of liberation from our enslavements and the healing of our wounds. As someone has incisively noted: Every sermon should touch where the hurt is, give the hurt a name, then point people in the direction of healing.

The truth is that congregations will be quite forgiving of occasional sub-par pulpit presentations, as long as our gospel is steadfastly hopeful and our caregiving consistently solid.

MINISTER AS PASTOR

DEVELOPING A CARING COMMUNITY

M y concept of ministry is **companioning**: walking hand in hand with our parishioners and others in joy and sorrow...being truly present in each relationship.

Betty Baker

Good ministers will walk with their people (young and old) to the ends of human trails, where footprints of pioneers grow dim and disappear, and there ministers will help save them from disillusionment, cynicism and despair, and lead them to take on the responsibilities of pioneering themselves.

Angus MacLean

Involvement with people is always a very delicate thing. It takes real maturity to become involved and not get all messed up.

Bernard Cooke

One seasoned minister was asked the three most important ingredients in her pastorate. Expecting her to list such indispensable elements as prayer, preaching, and scriptural study, the questioner was surprised when the minister answered: "First, I *visit* the people; second, I *counsel* the people; third, I *celebrate* the people."

The pastoral commission contends that people are primary in ministry. Clergy are summoned to love ideas and enjoy projects, but ministerial tasks are meaningful only when attached to people. Ministry is fundamentally the blessed privilege of entering and enjoying the precious places and moments of flesh-and-blood children, youth, and adults.

The words of Robert Raible, after a lifetime of ministry in Dallas, Texas, still hold:

> *There is only one rule for being an effective minister in the free church. It is to be fond of people. You needn't like some people, but you must love them all...If you cannot stand in the pulpit every Sunday, and look at your congregation and be able to say to yourself, 'I love every one of you, even though there are some of you whom I do not like', then you are useless as a parson...*

Or as Diana Heath puts it forcefully:

> *Maybe that is why ministers were invented. We may not minister all the time better than your neighbor who brings you chicken soup when you are sick, but we are reminders that such work ought be done in the world. Oh, yes, such work is never done. As a woman and a minister, I learned that a long time ago...*

Satisfying ministry occurs not only when clergy care about congregants, but also when we allow parishioners to return the favor. Pastoring constitutes the rhythm of giving and receiving, but ministers often fixate upon the first part of the equation. Clergy are usually reluctant to permit others to enter the heart of our lives, because we don't want to appear exposed or needy. Yet as poet Theodore Roethke phrased it: "Those who are willing to be vulnerable, move among mysteries."

What follows are some of the principles, and accompanying dragons, central to a pastoral ministry.

(I) Blessed Are They Who Mourn

A premier pastoring role is to enable people to rage and weep regularly and fully—"blessed are they who mourn, for they shall be comforted." Parishioners harbor an inordinate load of unresolved anguish. Consolation comes when we grieve openly and freely. Pastors are commissioned to assist their membership in diminishing both individual and communal sorrow through supportive catharsis.

It is staggering yet helpful to acknowledge the expanse of crises endured in every religious community—whether suburban, rural, or inner city. There are families beset with financial woes, terminal illnesses, or runaway youth. There are individuals burdened by chronic mental illness. Every week there are couples separating. There are members who are either victims or perpetrators of emotional, physical, or sexual abuse. There are parishioners currently hospitalized, grieving, disabled, facing overwhelming job pressures or loss of employment, home-bound or institutionalized, suffering a spiritual crisis or chemical dependency or wrestling valiantly in one recovery program or another.

There are individuals in every temple experiencing an unplanned pregnancy, or having to terminate one, or desperately seeking to get pregnant. Others are undergoing the birth or adoption of a child, while still others feel embattled as single parents. There are people who have been affected by accidental or natural disasters, been imprisoned or incurred the stress of moving to or from their home village. And there are always those in our beloved community who feel isolated, disoriented, despondent, and don't need professional help so much as spiritual comrades willing to be present, to call, to comfort, to hug.

The joke asks: "What job calls for indoor work with no heavy lifting?" The answer: "Ministry!" But that quip is only a half-truth. Ministers are generally exempt from heavy labor, although many of us, particularly in smaller congregations, have done more than our share of clerical and custodial work. However, parish ministry certainly includes ample emotional and spiritual lifting, weighty work to be sure. In an interdependent religious community, we can't be *responsible for* but we are profoundly *related to* one another's well-being.

(2) All Are Called to Be Caregivers

Where no counsel is, the people fall; but in the multitude of counselors, there is safety.

Proverbs II:I4

Every church is a community of revolving *careneeders* and *caregivers*. We urge one another to be strong enough to give care and vulnerable enough to receive care. To phrase it biblically, we are members, one with another. We are limbs of the same body, and, when there is an ache or loss, torment or separation in one of our limbs, the whole body shudders and rallies to restore equilibrium. If one of our arms gets caught in the door, then the other arm is needed to help set it free. We can rarely save one another from anguish, but we can regularly serve one another in the throes of it.

The classic notion that the pastoral work of the church is done totally, even predominantly, by the minister is bogus. Whereas congregants, in certain situations, desire the paid professional to be present with them, increasingly the pastor's job is to assist in the creation of a caregiving network wherein all church members can contribute equitably. The minister's job is not to **be** the saint but to **equip** the saints.

To phrase it in a slightly different way—clergy might do well to think of ourselves less as shepherds and more as sheep-dogs who regularly bark and nip at the heels of the sheep (although calling parishioners or anyone else "sheep" is a tricky image at best). The metaphor of the sheep-dog also reminds clergy that the bulk of our pastoral care is done on the move, coursing life's path, rather than through set visits or counseling sessions.

One of the most consequential reservoirs of compassion in contemporary church life has been the burgeoning of support groups for laity who bond together around a special need, such as grief recovery. Support groups spread the caregiving load around, reminding everyone, as Dick Gilbert states: "Caregiving is a calling, and all are called."

In the early stages of the Protestant Reformation it was John Calvin who inaugurated the parish call, demanding that ministers visit every church member at least once a year. That sounds pretty noble until you realize Calvin's reason for the parish call: to check up on the morals of the parishioners.

Twentieth-century laity can rest secure on two counts: Most modern ministers can't possibly get around to all the homes of congregants during one year; and when visiting, clergy will not be evaluating moral character—at least not with any calvinistic rigor. Needless to say, every church could benefit from the establishment of "A Caregiver's Network," where members share in overall church support and visitation. Two major benefits accrue. First, in serving, laity are always nourished themselves. Second, religious professionals neither grow overweening egos nor suffer burn out when some form of church-wide caregiver's network is in place.

(3) Paying Attention

Lyle Schaller, one of America's foremost church analysts, is convinced that the pastor's chief role, like that of an attending physician, is to be present. He states: "75% of the problems in congregational life stem from lack of attention to things and people!" As the Zen Buddhists offer: "Our most important human response is to pay attention, pay attention, pay attention."

But authentic caring is more complicated than that. Martin Buber tells of a student who came to him for counsel. Buber listened to his story and gave him professionally competent advice, and the student went away and took his own life. Buber goes on to tell how he searched to the core of his being as to whether if he had been really present, calm, and engaged, the outcome would have been the same.

Sometimes ministers are distant and disconnected from parishioners in need. We simply fail them. Occasionally, we clergy must be profoundly present, even physically so, as in the Old Testament story when the prophet Elisha is called upon to lay his own body over the body of a stricken boy and breathe his own breath into the boy's nostrils. When even prayer does not restore the child's health, Elisha's bodily closeness returns the lad to consciousness. In short, to be fully present as a minister often proves costly.

Yet, sometimes we give appropriately and to our utmost, and students still commit suicide and youngsters still die. Pastors are neither messiahs nor miracle workers. The renowned Carl Jung offers a sobering confession: "In my practice of psychiatry, I believe I have helped one-third of my patients, one-third registered no change, and one-third were worse as a result of psychoanalysis."

Furthermore, too many ministers burn out from excessive attentiveness to parishioners and inadequate responsiveness to family and self. Consequently, it is sometimes healthier for pastors to step back and aside, to bring counseling relationships to a conclusion, to refer parishioners to outside professionals, to let laity handle their own needs or engage in peer counseling with fellow congregants. Paying attention to congregants' singular soul-care needs will necessitate a prudent rhythm of being close and being apart. Responsive pastors are non-anxious absences as well as presences.

(4) Cultivating the Strengths of Laity

Dr. Karl Menninger, a pre-eminent therapist, taught his students to not only look for the problems patients brought to them but moreover to seek out the client's health and inner vigor. A church, while certainly caring about its own members, cannot become a hospital ward. A religious community should resemble a wellness center, catering to the energy and health of parishioners rather than extending their poverties and weaknesses. We are "care-fronters" who exhort those in need to identify, then embody, healing resources in their lives. Pastors will *lift* people but refuse to *carry* them.

Love, the genuine article, is not sentimental or mushy. Comforting members often means challenging them to take up their own pallets and walk as Jesus told the paralytic who had been stuck in his illness for three decades, refusing to enter the eddying pool for healing. Do you really want to be healed? is a bristly but fair question to ask some congregants. And the concomitant query we clergy must ask of ourselves is: Am I willing for my parishioners to be healed or do I need to remain enmeshed in co-dependent bonds?

(5) Caregiving is not Caretaking

There is a humbler tone both to the term and reality of **caregiver** than **caretaker**. The latter implies ministerial presumption to resolve or "take care of" a congregant's need.

Caretaking is both an impossible and undesirable route for pastors to pursue. Our mission as caregivers is to give steady, faithful succor in the face of a parishioner's stress and sorrow. Oliver Wendell Holmes captures the distinctions: "The physician's task is to *cure* rarely, *relieve* often, and *comfort* always." That's the pastor's role too. We cannot fix someone's soul; we can only enable them to live more gracefully and hopefully amidst their soul-ache.

Comfort means "to place one's strength alongside" another person, which is precisely what occurs in the Caregivers Network where laity place their vigor and might next to the weakness of fellow parishioners in need—on the phone, through notes, or in person. Caregivers are willing to be present, stand beside, be filled with fortitude, despite our own imperfections, since, lest we forget, clergy and laity are wounded healers anyway.

(6) Being Friends not Pals

The Old Druid was wise and sometimes a friend.
Michael Meade

There is a running debate among religious professionals as to whether we ought to become friends with parishioners. From my standpoint, it remains feasible to do so as long as each friendship bond acknowledges that clergy and laity share a professional relationship as well as an attendant power differential. Hence, there will be times when parishioner friends will need us in professional capacities such as counseling and rites-of-passage, including memorial service ministrations.

We clergy will be called upon not only to console parishioners but to confront them, occasionally pushing or pulling them into uncomfortable zones of consciousness. Pastors are indeed both mentors and tormentors, soothing encouragers as well as severe taskmasters who, at times, not unlike the

Zen *roshi* with student, deliver verbal slaps to the soul. Counterfeit pastors coddle congregants by telling them only the sweet things they hanker to hear.

Distinctions between being a friend and a pal must be preserved. I have participated for seven years in a men's support group that includes laity in our church, and whereas I am quite transparent and disclosing, there are lines I draw and boundaries I refuse to transgress. I never reveal anything that would put me or my wife (also, co-minister) in a compromising or compromised position or would vitiate my ability to minister satisfactorily to these men. Our friendships are close but not as intimate or freely open as might prove possible with buddies outside the church.

An additional wrinkle. When I am wrestling with a personal or marital dragon, I employ professional resources outside our congregation. I need a level of confidentiality and objectivity unattainable with member-friends in the parish.

(7) Receiving Ministry

> *The moment we fail to cling to one another, caress one another, and hold one another, the sea will engulf us and the light will go out.*
>
> James Baldwin

When ministers are willing to be on the receiving end of ministry, it broadens and strengthens the overall fabric of shared ministry. After twenty-eight years of professional ministry and seventeen years in the same church I conveyed the following sentiments in a sermon.

> *Albert Schweitzer used to salute all those people who, when our flame flickers some, show up and help rekindle the blaze once again. Well, from my perspective, those who rekindle our flickering flames minister to us, and I've ben-*

efited from countless rekindlers in this congregation since 1978. Did you know that I possess in my file cabinet a folder bulging with thoughtful and gracious notes of support that have sustained me during the "dark nights of my soul," such as when Carolyn's and my fathers died or when I had my arm surgeries? Those letters ministered to me.

And in the corner of my office have you noticed that I prominently display an album of notes and photos of affection presented to me by you, the members of this church, back in 1987, celebrating my 20th year in this strange, wondrous profession? I open it to a different page every week as a source of renewal along my ministerial path. Yes, you have ongoingly ministered to Carolyn and me in ways both vivid in your mind and in ways beyond your knowledge!

You have ministered to me and my family not only with agreeableness and light. You have cared enough to confront us when we have unnerved or ignored you. You have even forgiven us when we have inadvertently bruised you or undercut this clan we cherish in common.

And you haven't been the only ministers in my career. I remember the layperson at the outset of my ministry in our Pasadena church who came to my office after a blistering committee meeting to comfort me in my obvious distress. He embraced me and said: 'Tom, I didn't appreciate the position you took tonight, but you took quite a beating from our Board, and I want you to know that you can count on me never to leave the table or abandon you personally, whether or not we agree. You are my minister, and I hope to be one of yours!'

Another example of when I, the parish minister, was ministered to happened back in Davenport, Iowa in the early 1970s. We were struggling as a family to make ends meet, what with four children to support, Carolyn training to be a minister, and my salary not being all that substantial. In the midst of our financial tightness, a conservative banker and member of long-standing in our congregation came to me and blurted out: 'I want to be in charge of the pledge drive the next few years, and my first job will be to get your *salary up to where it belongs. I do this for your benefit and for mine as well.*

'Because when my family or I are having difficulties, and we need your ministry, the last thing I want is for my minister to be so strapped with financial stress or resentment that you will be of little value to us. You need our full support so you can be there fully for us!'

What a gift of ministry he gave me, our church, our entire living tradition of ministry.

Well, you get the point. In the dreary, lonely world of professional ministry, we clergy need the release of your wit and the restorative energy of your embrace. Deliver them both in ample measure. Never be shy with your humor or touch or criticism. And when you sense us growing stale, risk being a source of freshness in our ministry, or when you see us running too fast, invite us to slow down. And when we're off base, tell us the truth as you claim it. For our bond will continue to be a mutual blessing as long as we keep ministering to one another, back and forth, forth and back, all our days together!

MINISTER AS PROPHET

RESISTING AND RECONCILING

Hope has two beautiful daughters. Their names are anger and courage: anger at the way things are, and courage to see that they do not remain the way they are.

Augustine

I feel I have a duty to speak the truth as I see it and share not just my triumphs, not just the things that feel good, but the pain, the intense, often unmitigating pain. It is important to share how I know survival is survival and not just a walk through the rain.

Audre Lorde

On the whole, people do not achieve great moral heights out of a sense of duty...People must be charmed into righteousness. The language of aspiration rather than that of criticism and command is the proper pulpit language.

Reinhold Niebuhr

We have long held to the ideal of the priesthood of all believers, the idea that all believers have direct access to the ultimate resources of the religious life and that every believer has the responsibility of achieving an explicit faith. As an element of this radical laicism we need also the firm belief in the prophethood of all believers.

James Luther Adams

L ove is the polestar of ministry, and if it is exhibited in the pastoral commission toward members within the congregation, in the prophetic charge it extends outward to the larger community. As ministers we are summoned to share equally in loving inreach and outreach. Authentic compassion is indivisible. Social justice and interpersonal caregiving are as Siamese twins: when you tear them asunder, both wither and die.

Abraham Heschel wrote:

> *The prophet's word is a scream in the night. While the world is at ease and asleep, the prophet feels the blast from heaven...A prophet is chosen by God from on high; you cannot develop yourself into becoming a prophet. In contrast to being a great mystic or metaphysician, or philosopher, you can neither undergo formal external training, nor even inner purification to become a prophet. God chooses a prophet.*

Parish ministers seldom resemble Heschel's rarefied version of the prophet, since we are called as well to be inveterate institutionalists. Few parsons can roam the world as Jeremiahs and still hold down our daytime posts. Yet I have experienced the prophetic impulse at work in my own soul and in countless other clergy.

A prophet is not a foreteller or a soothsayer but a *forth*teller—someone who speaks truth to power and privilege and dares to blow the whistle on injustice at home, work, or play. Prophets refuse to remain on the sidelines as dispassionate spectators or cynics. They are spiritual warriors fierce with moral outrage, willing to confront all prevailing dragons.

Like the child of the fairy tale, prophets tell the emperors of the world that they wear no clothes. Like Sojourner Truth, prophets stand tall and speak undeniable truth against overwhelming odds: "Ain't I a woman?" Like Martin Luther, prophets publish the hypocrisy of sanctimonious autocrats. Like Rachel Carson, prophets shatter complacency and demand protection for earth's marginalized creatures. And as Richard Rohr reminds us:

> *There are two ways of being a prophet. One is to tell the enslaved that they can be free. It is the difficult path of Moses. The second is to tell those who think they are free that they are in fact enslaved. This is the even more difficult path of Jesus.*

Lest we wax romantic, remember that prophets are seldom appreciated by their peers. Prophets don't sign up for social action causes in order to be liked. Furthermore, many of us are very reluctant prophets. Jonah fled when God called him to preach repentance to the people of Nineveh. Only after three days of agonizing reflection in the belly of the whale was Jonah ready to be a forth-teller.

Prophets confront fraud, incompetence, abuse and other life-problems, not only in other communities or lands, but right in their own backyards, right where they live and love. And I need not convince us ministers that prophets are imperfect and impure, mixtures of goodness and evil ourselves.

(1) Raising Holy Hell

The prophetic dimension of ministry has been the hardest commission for me to actualize, being temperamentally a pliant and conciliatory spirit. I recently made a public vow that for the final laps of my ministry I would be keener in recognizing when my harmonious inclinations are but a chicken's clothing in disguise, when my fence-sitting serves as cowardice, when my incessant reflection bespeaks faintheartedness, when my taking a firm stand would prove the better part of sound doctrine and solid ministry.

I entered the ministry essentially to build some heaven but

have realized that raising some hell is also integral to this craft. As my ministerial consciousness matures, I increasingly own the rootage of the radical wing of the Protestant Reformation in its charge for us to be protesters: to name demons, confront injustices, enter skirmishes born of a resolute conscience.

Whereas my personal ministerial dragon has been my reluctance to raise hell, the dragon frustrating some clergy is their inability to abate their hell-raising. There are those ministers who engage in misplaced spanking and unresolved volcanic rage under the guise of being honorably indignant. As colleague David Pohl sagely states: "You can get angry as a minister, but if you lose your temper, you are likely to lose your influence as well." Needless to say, we all have various dragons to shake hands with in fulfilling our mission as prophetic ministers.

(2) Discernment

When I was in the formative stages of my ministry, I was taught something that has held me in good stead ever since: "As a minister you are not compensated for all the hours you put in so much as paid for making wise judgments. It is not a question of how many things you do but rather finding the right things to do at the right time. You simply never work for hours but for objectives." Judgment is critical in all phases of ministry, most definitely in the prophetic area.

There are thousands of worthy causes clamoring for our ministerial resources. Some won't mesh with our peculiar talents or interests. Some will suck us dry. So, the critical virtue for the minister as prophet is "discernment," homing in on concerns that truly rouse our enthusiasm and answering cries that we might be able to handle now. Beware of the temptation to sacrifice ourselves with an overload of "do-gooding." Ministers must adroitly sidestep the salvation-by-merits racket.

But it's not so easy for bona fide religious activists, since we desire to do everything at once. Sidney Harris deftly distinguished the respective plights of the conservative and the liberal. A conservative throws a 25-foot rope to a person who is drowning 50 feet from shore and then encourages her to swim the other half for the good of her character. A liberal on the other hand throws a 50 foot rope to a person drowning 25 feet from shore but then lets go of the rope and walks away to address the next fashionable cause.

The key for prophetic ministers is to set communal and personal limits and priorities—to turn our abundance of sugary platitudes into a few stout acts and avoid becoming another grim, ground-down ministerial crusader. Here are some directives: (1) Focus attention on one or two matters that match up with your heart; (2) Choose issues upon which you can have impact and see some tangible rewards within a reasonable period of time; (3) Choose projects that require creative action; (4) Establish realistic goals and follow through on them; (5) Spend time around *organizers* rather than *agonizers*—people who lift your spirit, fire your mind, spur your conscience; and (6) Remember you and your family are "worthy causes" too.

(3) Serving in Different Ways

At the height of U.S. involvement in Southeast Asia, William Sloane Coffin, pastor of New York City's Riverside Church and a card-carrying radical, was one of a group of ministers who urged Henry Kissinger to withdraw U.S. troops. Mr. Kissinger, pushing them on the complexities of such a proposal, asked, "How would YOU get the boys out of Vietnam?" To which Coffin, turning to the prophet Amos, responded, "Mr. Kissinger, our job is to proclaim that 'justice must roll down like waters and righteousness like a mighty stream.' Your job is to work out the details of the irrigation system."

Ministers and legislators have different domains of accountability to be sure, yet the separation between the prophetic and the political can not be so cleverly differentiated anymore. Ministers dare not pontificate without getting our hands dirty. There are various ways to execute our prophetic responsibility in the public sphere. Some clergy will choose to do it primarily through social *education*, others social *service*, still others through social *witness*, and, finally, there are those who will specialize in social *action*. Ministers ought to become ambidextrous, varying their prophetic tactics and responses.

Whatever our prophetic mode of operation, ministers need to quit comparing ourselves with Hosea or Dorothy Day, Confucius or Harriet Tubman and, instead, remain true to our own version of prophetic participation.

(4) Sharing the Burden and the Recognition

Sometimes we ministers fail to equalize prophetic loads and rewards with congregants, reserving prophecy as some sacrosanct niche for ourselves. Or ministerial jealousy sets in when lay members are more involved than we are in being guardians of righteousness either in the larger community or in their places of work. But the dragons of insecurity or envy serve no useful purpose. Remember the Old Testament story (Numbers 11:26-29) where it says:

> *Now two men remained in the camp, one named Eldad, and the other named Medad, and the spirit rested upon them; they were among those registered, but they had not gone out to the tent, and so they prophesied in the camp. And a young man ran and told Moses, 'Eldad and Medad are prophesying in the camp.' And Joshua the son of Nun, the minister of Moses, one of his chosen men, said: 'My lord Moses, forbid them.' But Moses said to him, 'Are you jealous for my sake? Would that all the Lord's people were prophets, that the Lord would put his spirit upon them!'*

Again, the role of the parish minister is primarily to enlist fellow congregants in the ranks of the "prophethood of all believers." As Bill Gardiner directs ministerial leaders: "A significant number of church members are involved in doing prophetic ministry in the world. Give them a break. Encourage them to live balanced lives. Empower them."

One of the most meaningful Sundays of our worshiping year is when we have various laity, four at a time, share their stories of faith-in-action as exemplified in their personal and vocational lives. The testimonies are motivational, since they publicly demonstrate that the prophetic load in every congregation can and must be fully shared. During this same worship service, we also present our annual Shameless Agitator Award to the church member who best personifies the spirit of one of our deceased comrades who unabashedly promoted social causes throughout his lifetime.

One of our recent spokespersons, Lynn Eldred, stated her prophetic witness powerfully:

> *I have my own metaphor for social change work. We all have a pocketful of puzzle pieces, representing the skills and experiences we contribute to the common good. I can pocket my pieces hoarding them, or play them. If I do a cost-benefit analysis of working for social justice, I might never play these pieces, because it takes a leap of faith to step up to the table of history and say, 'I'm willing to commit myself to making changes.'*
>
> *There are no guarantees, and we can't see the cover of the box to know where to place the pieces or see how the pattern will come out. To play these pieces means to play with faith, knowing that we may never even see the frame constructed in our lifetime. Perhaps some of the puzzles I work on will never be completed. But I need to play my pieces anyway.*
>
> *The beauty of our Church is that there are so many tables on which to play your pieces: the environment, peace,*

the homeless, children in Tijuana, social justice causes world-wide, AIDS in our community, anti-racist work, gay and lesbian issues, reproductive rights and more. It is a powerful statement that this work springs from our community, because my pieces mean nothing unless they're connected, in synergy with others...because there is a forging of powerful bonds when a group of individuals pool their pieces and find that, together, they have constructed a portion of the sky or a section of the field.

We all have pieces to contribute. We can pocket our pieces or risk failure in hopes of contributing towards changing history. My life has been immeasurably enriched when I have taken that risk.

(5) Avoiding the Path of False Prophecy

False prophets tend to deal in absolutes: "You aren't moral if, you aren't religious unless..." Beware of such false prophets. They dwell everywhere, even within our own well-intentioned ministerial consciences. The authentic prophet aspires to declare: "My action is no more and no less than my action. It may not be yours. I cannot equate my gambles with the goals of the gods. I will not pontificate from pulpits or committees or resolutions or marketplaces or anywhere else. I will offer my convictions and will listen in love to the prophet in every person, both within and outside my congregation."

The Old Testament prophet Jeremiah knew what he was talking about when he warned humanity that there are any number of false prophets roaming about, "healing the wounds lightly" and preaching "peace, peace when there is no peace." (Jeremiah 6:14). The minister as prophet reminds people not to be spiritual zombies but to stay concerned and involved. The religious journey is not supposed to make us feel good but to do good, to be compassionate rather than remain complacent.

Prophetic exemplars are balanced as peace-makers, justice-builders, and joy-sharers.

(6) Hissing without Biting

The progressive African-American minister Howard Thurman tells of a certain village whose population was being destroyed by the periodic attacks of a cobra. At length, a holy person came to the village, and the plight of the people was made known to her. Immediately, she sought the snake, to urge it to discontinue its destruction. The snake cautiously agreed to leave the villagers alone.

Days passed; the villagers discovered the snake was no longer dangerous. The word went from person to person: "Hey, the cobra does not bite any more. Something has happened to the cobra. The cobra does not bite any more." Almost overnight the attitude of everyone changed. The fear of the cobra disappeared and, in its place, there developed a daring boldness. All sorts of tricks were played on the cobra; its tail was pulled, water was thrown on it, little children threw sticks and bits of stone at the cobra.

There was no attempt to take its life by any direct means, only a number of petty annoyances and cruelties which, when added up, rendered the snake's existence increasingly perilous. It was nearly dead when the holy woman came back through the village. With great bitterness, the cobra implored, "I did as you commanded me; I stopped striking the villagers and now see what they have done to me. What must I do?"

The holy woman replied: "But you did not obey me fully. It is true that I told you not to bite the people, but I did not tell you not to HISS at them!"

Being positively, resolutely angry—neither passive-aggressive nor hostile—is an essential gift in effective ministry. Call it healthy hissing or compassionate confrontation, prophetic clergy need to practice it. As hissers we are charged to kick our kin out of smugness and contentment. We create sufficient ruckus in our ministerial posts so that goodness, excellence, and righteousness might be served. A smooth, honeyed ministry ought never to be our goal.

Our world desperately desires to venture alternatives to both bloodshed and passivity, to practice what Gandhi called *satyagraha*, which translates as "soul or truth force." Every conflict or problem, whether among family or friends, between communities or governments, will be addressed ultimately either through violent or nonviolent force. Those who choose nonviolent force are courageous risk-takers who opt for the force of justice, of love, of redistributing power, of noncooperation, of relentless resistance to evil, of imaginative, revolutionary ideas. Prophetic ministers aspire to be forceful carriers and promoters of "satyagraha."

(7) Confronting Our Own Evil

We must never resist evil as if it only exists outside ourselves. The demons of greed and indignity need to be confronted within as well as without our own souls. As one minister put it: Speaking truth to power is particularly challenging when you yourself are holding the power.

We are prone as prophetic ministers to be unduly concerned with cleansing the world of injustice and fail to face the wrongs and inequities in our own office or household. Alice Walker went right to the heart of the matter when she wrote:

> When Martin (Luther King, Jr.) said, 'Agitate nonviolently against unjust oppression, I assumed he meant in the home, if that's where the oppression was.'

MINISTER AS PRIEST

HONORING LIFE'S SACRED PASSAGES

W*orship has the primary place in religion because it unites whereas beliefs divide.*

Von Ogden Vogt

Always there remains this need to explain to each other that we are good. The individual person needs this, the whole human race needs a Yea, needs the ceremonial pat on the back that says: 'Come on, come, we can make it!'

Corita Kent

Worship is the practice of giving ourselves over to the healing powers which govern our destinies. In worship we dedicate ourselves to the transforming powers of life. In worship we bow down before the powers of our destiny.

Frank Carpenter

The classic definition of priest or priestess is "one who offers sacrifice." Sacrifice is the process by which something is "made holy." Ministers are called to render existence sacred through all we do, including rituals of meaning and empowerment. Our priestly challenge is to assure that personal transitions and congregational encounters are sacramental in the broadest and deepest senses.

As earthly mediators between the human and divine realms, priests pay radical attention both to worship **and** to rites-of-passage. The word worship derives from the Anglo-Saxon *"weorth-scipe,"* which literally means **shaping matters of worth**. Therefore, priests order and shape the liturgical flow so that moments of sustaining value might transpire for the gathered community. It is tempting to fall into the trap of worshiping our work, working at our play, and playing at our worship. The healthiest rhythm in the religious life is to work at work, play at play and worship at worship, realizing that occasional mixes and crossovers will prove necessary and nourishing.

In our priestly functions, we are also ritual guides. Laboring in tandem with laity, clergy create effective rituals that recognize and uphold people through the multifarious passages of our lives. Some rites will focus on *individuals* (memorial services), others on the entire *church community* (the laying of a cornerstone), and still others on *society* as a whole (the Martin Luther King, Jr. parade and celebration), or the entire *cosmos* (Earth Day). Priests are commissioned to ask: What are the momentous occasions that people experience in life and how can our faith-community ceremonialize them with staying power?

(I) Relying upon the Spirits

Worship services must reach deeper, soar higher, and generate compassion more broadly than just mingling clever words with touching sentiments. Ministers need to create solid and enduring religious growth, not Sunday highs. A sense of holiness instead of goose bumps. In Hinduism one goes to worship for "seeing;" hence, Buddha charged his disciples to "come and see." The Jewish approach invites us to "come and hear." Seeing and hearing, feeling and touching, tasting and smelling are mutually reinforcing in robust worship that addresses the needs of the whole person.

At its finest, worship can do for the spirit what sleep does for the body. It can strengthen, renew, invigorate our lives. It can *inspire*, "breathe fresh life" into our beings. However, we minister-priests harbor no illusions. We can't just say: "Hey, let's do worship or let's be worshipful today!" After all, the last Major League baseball player to hit .400 did so in 1941. Ted Williams was his name. Both priests and parishioners ought to be well-pleased with a batting average somewhere in the .300s. There are too many variables, both human and divine, to forecast glib predictions. Mystery cannot be manipulated. Reverence cannot be programmed. Worship is ultimately a matter of grace.

I remember one of the Presbyterian ministers in my adolescence claiming that he conducted worship as if it depended upon the Holy Spirit, but he prepared as if it banked upon his own effort. That's how the process goes. We create the conditions under which worship might transpire, and then the holy spirits take over.

(2) Recognizing Liturgy as the People's Work

One of the most treacherous dragons tormenting the priest is our own arrogance combined with the parishioners' assumption that worship belongs to the minister. Not so. Liturgy or *leitourgia* literally means "the work of the people." Public worship is fundamentally not presentation but participation. Congregants need to be involved not merely by worshiping from their pews or by coming forward to receive the sacraments but also through offering personal songs, prayers, credos, and homilies. The classic notion of the priesthood of all *believers* really needs to be reframed to signify the priesthood of all *contributors*.

We call our Sunday gatherings *worship services* for two reasons: first, everyone is called upon to be a server during worship; and, second, service is demanded at the close of the worship. Our celebrations issue in consecrated lives.

(3) Ordering Worship

The most emotionally accurate, spiritually profound, community-shared order of service can never promise a worshipful hour. The experience of worship remains ineffable.

Nonetheless, priests are avid believers in the liberating effects of order. We are convinced that in all areas of religious life, worship included, freedom is not the gift of formlessness but resides in the fulfillment of form. Structure, when sensitively conceived and executed, awakens meaning. Framework gives birth to flexibility.

An order of worship need not be either inchoate or inflexible, but it must be responsive to the moods of the human spirit. Worship categories signal outward expressions of the soul's inner stirrings. If the movements prove to be organic and vital, they will endure. If not, they should be modified, even replaced. The major elements of the order of service we use in our San Diego church are:

Centering or traveling within to a place of quiet and depth;
Affirming Community or recognizing our irrevocable bond with God, one another, and the entire creation;
Proclaiming Hope or declaring the possibilities despite the limits of human existence;
Returning to the Service of Life or committing ourselves to a more just and loving world given the inspiration we have just experienced;

Sharing Fellowship, or the opportunity to embrace our spiritual kin before heading for home.

Let's briefly explore each one. The **Centering** segment of worship marks when congregants cross over the threshold and enter the sanctuary. Some enter fifteen minutes ahead, others race in breathlessly on the hour, still others arrive late. Whenever worshipers enter our Meeting House, they are encouraged to center their being and prepare for a special appointment with the "still, small voice." The deeper we travel within, the quieter we are, the more likely we are to encounter the Source of all existence.

The word for sabbath in Hebrew comes from the root meaning: "to desist." Centering exhorts us to cease the scattered pace and activity of our days, if but for a short while. We are invited to catch our breath, to honor the Sabbath and to keep it holy by worshiping alone...together. These brief centering moments remind congregants to renew themselves throughout the week with additional periods of stillness and silence.

During the Centering time there are three aids to one's own natural meditation: organ music, a scriptural text in the order of service, and an opportunity for reverentially lighting a candle in a trencher at the front of the sanctuary while recalling a moment or person in sadness, celebration, and gratitude.

Affirming Community reminds us that through words of welcome, the ringing of the singing bowl, the lighting of the flaming chalice by one of our church children, and through gathering music that we are summoned to communal worship. We are not celebrating in utter solitude on a mountaintop somewhere, as awe-inspiring as that might be, but we have intentionally convened as an intergenerational community in the presence of the Eternal Spirit that dwells within, among, and beyond us. As Clarke Wells would remind us:

The church is to the single self what the belly of a guitar is to the single string. The single string unconnected, iso-

*lated, alone, is twangy, weak, somewhat pitiful; but when
tied to a good frame and resonating with others, it becomes
in Browning's words 'not a fourth sound, but a star.'*

It is often said that since ministers have to be thoroughly
organized and somewhat detached leaders, it is impracticable
for us to be worshipers ourselves on Sunday. It is surely difficult but not impossible. There are ample moments of silence,
song, as well as actual lay leadership when we minister-priests
can drink from the wellsprings of soulful refreshment. Shared
liturgy can present real and vital experiences for both pulpit
and pew; in fact, congregational worship constitutes one of
the rare places in society today where there is no editor or
sponsor or medium intervening. Hence, there are plenty of
times when we come to church out of sorts, broken,
unexpectant and unreceptive, and then, an epiphanous moment stirs our depths. We come out of habit and our souls are
lovingly sideswiped.

The middle movement of the morning worship service is
designated **Proclaiming Hope** and signifies religion's un-
swerving tribute to the possibilities of human existence amid
its inevitable barriers and losses. Be it Jewish or Hindu, Buddhist or Christian, Moslem or Universalist, the gospel at the
core of authentic worship must carry an encouraging message
that transforms the seemingly unyielding anguish of reality.

This worship segment declares "good news" through *read-
ings*—humorous, weighty, or poignant—from secular sources
and the world's religious literature, and through choral or
instrumental *music*—a dimension of worship that taps regions
of the soul unvisited by any other mode of communication.
When surveyed concerning what moves worshipers most
deeply, congregants invariably mention certain songs or mu-
sical offerings.

The Credo segment, which we added a few years back in
our community worship, is decidedly one of the most evoca-

tive and worthful contributions during the entire hour. Women and men in our congregation representing distinct backgrounds, areas of church involvement, and theological persuasions, share the heart of their religious odysseys and values. They testify in five minutes (remembering that it is harder to write a short piece than a long one) to what our particular faith community means in their evolving religious pilgrimage. *Credo* literally indicates what "I give my heart or loyalty to," a formulation that takes the presenter beneath intellectual assent and beyond customary belief.

Sermons should be seen as central not dominant events within the worship process. They are valiant yet flawed efforts to wrestle with the angels and dance with the dragons awake in our beings. It is prudent for preachers to emulate Abraham Lincoln's observation: "When I hear ministers preach, I like to see them act as if they were fighting bees."

Through meditation and prayer, worshipers have the chance to consolidate the morning's wisdom, to seek guidance from immanent and transcendent sources, to offer thanks and adoration, to declare joys and sorrows, to confess and be forgiven, to be emboldened for life's struggle. Whatever the worship theme for the morning might be, pastoral prayers remain a constant source of consolation for congregants, especially those in no emotional shape to hear, let alone obey, the gospel's chastening challenge for the day. Indeed, if silent and spoken prayer hem the fabric of the entire service, it will be far less likely to unravel. Some folks have bravely ventured forth from depths of despond, arriving at our worshiping home, hungry for spiritual sustenance. We priests stand that morning among the instruments through whom the Great Spirit can assuage pain and transform loss. A worship service wanting in comfort and reassurance is unredemptive.

In addition to faith and works, every religious institution requires financial resources to support all we cherish and hold dear. The practice of a freewill, corporate offering keeps the flame of spiritual enlightenment and prophetic witness burning brightly. Passing the plates is both financially prudent and sound doctrine for the endurance of a faith community. Giving money during the service constitutes an act of worship.

The fourth rubric of worship is called **Returning to the Service of Life**. At the close of every worship gathering we rededicate our lives to serving our universe and all inhabitants therein.

A Sunday worship filled with harmonic convergence means little unless the substance and spirit we shared inside the sanctuary are translated into service in the larger world. This movement marks the time for each of us, in our own ways, to turn rites into deeds, to march forth to alter our inner and outer worlds, surrounded by a tribe of comrades to whom we can turn for goading and comfort when our consciences chicken out or our spirits flag.

We can't serve satisfactorily without worshipping, and we don't truly worship without then serving. William Penn took a friend to his Quaker Meeting. They sat for an hour in silence, and the friend turned to Penn and asked, "Well, when does the service begin?" Penn firmly replied, "The service begins when the meeting ends."

Sunday morning worship concludes with **Sharing Fellowship** together on the patio—enjoying a restorative sampling of human touch, activity enlistment, and commingling of the intergenerational community—fortified by refreshments, sometimes luncheon programs.

There is a New Testament admonition that urges religious pilgrims to worship in "spirit and truth." To worship with exuberance and vitality or *spirit* in conjunction with sincerity and congruence or *truth*. Spirit without truth produces sentimental drivel. Truth without spirit is effete. A religious community gathers to worship in spirit and truth—to experience life more abundantly that we might in turn share it more mightily.

(4) Collaborating in Imaginative Rituals

In addition to being worship leaders, minister-priests are also involved with parishioners in establishing meaningful rites of transition. The primary dragon lurking in these waters is the challenge to be a central, but not dwarfing, figure in the development and delivery of rituals. As with worship leadership, a responsive priest is more enabler and collaborator than sole director.

Religion is a covenantal adventure, and rituals are only accurate and meaningful when shaped in tandem by clergy and laity. The role of the priest is to challenge individuals, couples, and families, assisting them in the articulation of their heartfelt convictions, whether planning a memorial service or their 30th anniversary of vows.

The classic rites—from baptisms to marriages to funerals—must be revisioned, lest they become rote and grow stale. Each religious tradition is challenged to pour new wine into its familiar wine skins. **Tradition** signals that something has been passed on to us, and we pledge to manage it with creative care while it resides in our hands, then pass it on afresh to the next generation.

It is integral to our priestly responsibilities to fashion rites of passage that capture the spirit of our times as well as satisfy the needs of our local congregations. In our church, for several years now, we have paid homage to our various configurations of families. We designate it the Wholly Family Service, and the entire range of home-constellations—from traditional, to gay and lesbian partnerships, to single adults with animals, to blended families, to individuals for whom the church is a family—are celebrated and given the opportunity to testify concerning their singular unit.

We also hallow life-transitions such as graduations, retirements, name-changes, relational dissolutions, and ceremonies for members when they leave our church community.

Following is our Litany-of-Farewell:

If you must part from us, may God lead you to beautiful places. Know that when you depart we will never forget you. And know when you return we will never have enough of you!

Sufi blessing

Leader:

In our church traditions we would do well to celebrate exits as well as entrances...welcoming with warmth and saying good-bye with gratitude. Not just privately and individually but also publicly and corporately. Today we share a rite-of-transition for our church companions who will be leaving our premises but not our heritage, our presence, but not our lives.

All:

Tom and Susan (parents), Max and Catherine (children), we are genuinely sad that you are departing our church community. In your own singular ways each of you has enriched our beloved church. We will miss your various gifts.

We know ourselves to be a people of exodus, pilgrims on a journey. We acknowledge that our religious existence is one of continual dyings and rebirths, beginnings and endings, movings and relocations. And yet, we are still shaken every time any one of our tribe leaves this particular home. Such commencements bring us both sorrow and joy.

May you parting be a good one. May your relocation be gratifying. And may you find another sanctuary of "free-thinking mystics with hands" to strengthen your spirit along its path.

For what you have been for us, thank you. For what you might become for others elsewhere, yes. We give you our blessings. We send you forth with faith and hope and love.

Then each family member has an opportunity to share their own words of memory and thanksgiving.

MINISTER AS POLITICIAN

CREATING AND SUSTAINING COMMUNITY

G od save us clergy from petering out into simply great executives.

H. M. S. Richards

Do not fear power but fear its misuse; do not damn power, but condemn its inordinate concentration.

William Jones

I want to be with people who submerge in the task, who go into the fields to harvest and work in a row and pass the bag along. Who stand in the line and haul in their places, who are not parlor generals and field deserters but move in a common rhythm when the food must come in or the fire be put out.

Marge Piercy

As long as I live, I lead, but I never substitute a leadership role for zestful living.

Charlie Kreiner

Many poets say they are not political. If a tree said that, it would be more convincing than when humans say it.

Robert Bly

The choice before us is not whether we will be prophetic or bureaucratic. We must learn how to be prophetic bureaucratically.

Robert Spike

U nder the commission of politician, I want to focus upon two central regions: minister as empowering-leader and minister as community-builder.

EMPOWERING-LEADERS

The root meaning of the term *power* comes from the Latin *posse*, "to be able." When Nietzsche proclaimed: "Wherever I found the living, there I found the will to power," he was implying that humans fulfill ourselves through demonstrating our able-ness, through wielding the might with which we have been blessed. To actualize our god-given power, then, is the basic charge delivered to us upon birth. As Emerson remarked: "Do the thing and you shall have the power. But they who do not the thing, have not the power."

Leadership is a craft. Here again, the roots of the word are helpful. *Craft* comes from the German word *kraft*, meaning power or strength. Leadership demands the sensitive and wise handling of craft or power. But power, per se, is amoral. It can be used, as can physical energy and nuclear force, for good or bad ends. Power comes with the territory of being human. It is the ability to cause, prevent, or receive change.

The church or temple is not primarily a refuge from the storm or even a house of enlightenment or embrace; we are fundamentally a place of empowerment. As spiritual sisters and brothers on the path of truth-seeking, justice-building, and joy-sharing, we boldly say to one another:

> *Come on, you can open your heart to love, you can surrender your soul to anguish, you can expand your mind to wisdom, you can lift your spirit in aspiration, you can declare your conscience in service, you can treat your body as a temple. You are able. You are a powerful being. In this church and through our programs you can utilize your power in pursuit of the good, the true, and the beautiful. Here you can be who you really are and grow to become whom you*

desire to become. On this holy ground you can speak with authority and act with conviction!

Let me be more specific.

Empowering (not empowered where control remains vested in certain individuals) leaders keep the gift of power moving around the room. They don't drain authority from others, as a tyrant does, but rather enliven all whom they touch. Buddha, the awakened one, was an empowering presence because he nudged those whom he met along the path to stay keen, growing, generative, awake.

Empowering leaders are also willing to be assertive and stand accountable when necessary. Robert Frost has a lengthy poem with a drawn out title called: "How Hard It Is to Keep from Being King When It's in You and in the Situation." There are definitely times when we ministers have been appointed or chosen to serve as the equivalent of queens or kings. We know, and everyone else in the temple knows, that being the leader is in us and in the situation. We spurn such leadership status at great cost both to our souls and to the welfare of an entire religious community. Empowering leaders display neither cockiness nor false modesty but egos of the proper size for given contexts.

Yet different occasions summon different modes of leadership. Empowering leaders make the necessary adjustments. The crisis of mere subsistence on a life-raft requires one type of leader. Democratic stability and compromise call for another. Revolutionary activity for still a third.

Most importantly, empowering leaders don't hanker to horde power. They share it as in a jazz combo that comprises a harmonious, mutually supportive, creative alliance of soloists.

A healthy congregation need never pit its clout against that of the clergy. The converse is likewise valid. In fact, true religious community demands co-equality of power. Empowering church leaders are neither jealous nor frightened to divide the burdens or share the glory. When parsons claim that *we* have to start and finish most every church project, we may, in fact, be betraying our reluctance to permit laity to shoulder certain jobs.

Much is demanded of clergy and tasks are seldom completed, but we can also become egomaniacs, neither allowing laity to push and pull their full weight nor letting God do God's fair share. Bishop Templeton would regularly chastise himself as a workaholic by acknowledging that God was trying to get through to him: "You can sleep now, Bishop. I'll watch for a while!"

The empowering leader is wakeful, resolute, shares power, and knows when to surrender privilege and invite change. A phrase from the political philosopher John Locke is germane: "Power is the ability to cause **or** receive change." Usually, leaders are depicted as change-agents alone but seldom portrayed as those brave enough to *receive* change. Yet an empowering presence is ambidextrous: displaying the capacity both to catalyze and welcome change.

Another related feature. The unthreatened leader is one who is willing to reside under the power and authority of others rather than constantly holding sway at the top of the mountain. The good leader can be a good follower. Remember the humorous quote attributed to Disraeli: "Hey, I must follow the people, for I am their leader!"

It's disturbing to recognize that thousands of books have been written on leadership and none on the art of followership. Countless college presidents have told their students that schools are meant to train leaders. I have rarely heard anyone profess to train followers. Yet both are required to create and sustain a vital religious enterprise.

The empowering leader is balanced, knowing when to step out front, when to take up the rear, and when to walk side-by-side. They think of themselves as communal stewards rather than special owners. In short, the empowering leader is a servant. Ministers as servant-leaders show soiled hands, bruised hearts and skinned knees, because rather than leading from a distance, they are embroiled in the daily fracases of building a vital and beloved community. There is a delightful reminiscence of Ralph Waldo Emerson as a child. He was watching a lumberjack sawing up some wood. The task was beyond young Waldo's strength, but finally he saw a way to be useful. "May I," asked Emerson, "do some grunting for you?"

In Herman Hesse's story *Journey to the East* we see a band of people on a mythical trek, probably Hesse's own spiritual quest. The central figure of the story is Leo accompanying the party as the servant who does their servile chores, but who also sustains them with his spirit and song. He is a person of extraordinary presence and appeal. All goes well until Leo disappears. Then the group falls aparts, and the journey is dropped.

The narrator, one of the party, after some years of wandering finds Leo and is taken into the order that had sponsored the journey. There he discovers that Leo, whom he had known first as servant, was in fact the titular head of the order, its guiding spirit and honorable leader. A classic example of minister as empowering leader-servant.

And remember one of our superior twentieth-century religious guides, another servant-leader, Dr. Martin Luther King, Jr., who offered these inspirational sentiments in his closing sermon:

> *If any of you are around when I have to meet my day, I don't want a long funeral. And if you get somebody to deliver the eulogy, tell them not to talk too long. Tell them not to mention that I have a Nobel Peace Prize. That isn't important....I'd like someone to mention that day that Martin Luther King, Jr. tried to give his life serving others. I'd like*

for somebody to say that Martin Luther King, Jr. tried to love somebody...And I want you to say that I tried to love and serve humanity.

COMMUNITY-BUILDERS

M inisters as politicians are also summoned to be community-builders. A "politician" literally is one who assists in producing and maintaining the *polis*, the ancient Greek city-state. A church community constitutes the equivalent of a *polis* and the minister as politician is commissioned, under the direction and alongside the companionship of laity, to embody certain principles in sustaining the temple as polis.

Psychologist Scott Peck, in his trenchant book *In the Different Drum*, makes pivotal distinctions between pseudo and genuine community. He sees pseudo-community as a smug collective where members seek instant gratification or as an inchoate tribe of wanderers grazing the land without settling down. Genuine community, on the other hand, is a growing connection that requires energy, time, commitment, evolution; it is activated by affectional bonds rather than static rules.

Community doesn't happen by merely wanting or praying for it, but through intentionally re-seeing it daily. Here are some of the bedrock principles essential to generative religious community.

(I) Vigilance

Gordon McKeeman reminds us that the derivation of the word community, although related to communion and communication, comes more specifically from the Latin MUNIO meaning "to arm." Therefore, with the prefix COM, meaning "together," community actually occurs wherever there is shared growth and security, a context of mutual assistance and vigilance.

Religious community is thus composed of compassionate arms. Arms are engaged in firm yet friendly wrestling matches rather than blood-baths or back-stabbing. Arms huddle together in times of anguish and swing open in rejoicing. Arms reach outward in justice-building and peace-making, not merely inward in narcissistic embrace.

In genuine religious community arms are watchful to guard against any behavior that would undermine the covenantal values. Church members, both laity and religious professionals, defend one another against pomposity and shallowness, outside agitators or internal saboteurs.

(2) Reflecting Backward and Marching Forward

> To acknowledge our ancestors, means we are aware that we did not make ourselves, that the line stretches all the way back, perhaps, to God; or to Gods. We remember them because it is an easy thing to forget; that we are not the first to suffer, rebel, fight, love and die. The grace with which we embrace life, in spite of the pain, the sorrows, is always a measure of what has gone before.
>
> Alice Walker

Durable religious community doesn't merely dwell in the present moment: it travels back and forth in time, honoring those comrades who have gone before us and bequeathing those yet to be born the gift of tomorrow. Congregations should regularly remember their dead (noting that the biblical phrase for dying means "to be gathered to one's people") and salute turning points of their common history without getting mired in the past. Every Easter morning in our church we prayerfully read the names of those in our parish who have been born and those who have died during the previous year. It furnishes one of the significant sacraments of our ongoing, communal existence.

(3) Honoring the Law of Respectfulness

There's a really big law that we have to obey. That law is respect. We have to treat everything with respect. The earth, the animals, the plants, the sky. Everything.

Catherine Attla

In weaving a sturdy and resilient web of religious community, we pay tribute to circles of power and meaning that permeate the entire ecosphere, be they plants or animals, deities or humans. As pilgrims committed to radical interdependence we promote global unity as a biological fact and our religious aspiration.

Respect means "to look at something or someone again and again." Respect is the only virtue sizable enough to hold the "wholly other" caringly in our sight, recognizing, along with Elisabeth Schussler Fiorenza, that our commission as community-builders is to "forge a discipleship of equals."

Following his wrestling match with soul-deep temptations, Jesus, armed with the power of the Spirit, returned to Nazareth, the home of his upbringing, went to the synagogue and on the sabbath day read the lesson from Isaiah, "to bring good tidings to the afflicted." This testament-bridging message of unconditional regard for the marginalized of society, was for Jesus the determinative feature of discipleship. He said: "If you love one another, then you are my followers." He didn't say: "If you are wealthy, bright, emotionally stable, good looking, or cling to me, then you are my followers."

The early Christian Church was described as *koinonia*: a fellowship of partners who shared in the spirit through spreading love. Authentic koinonia or religious community consists of members gazing not inwardly but extending outwardly. Hence, spiritual growth is never exhausted by private disciplines, however carefully honed, but spurs us forth to incarnate respectfulness among all living entities—starting now, starting nearby.

(4) Declaring the Meeting Open

> *Behold, I set before you an open door, which no one is able to shut.*
>
> Revelations 3:8

A well-built yet pliant religious polis is responsive to the outsider whether arriving with gifts or coming empty-handed. For "hospitality to strangers is greater than reverence for the name of God," recounts the Hebrew proverb, and the New Testament confirms the same sentiment when it declares: "I was a stranger and you took me in."

African-American poet June Jordan cuts to the quick when she asserts: "My hope is that our lives will declare this meeting open." Religious communities don't have a very good track record with diversity. While tolerating differences of conviction, color, class, and capability in theory, we still gravitate, in practice, toward homogeneity of lifestyle, social behavior, and rituals. We are tightly tribal rather than expansively communal.

Three emphatic reminders on our quest to constructing a strong yet supple web of inclusion:

> *—If we dwell in a community that is comfortable, then it's probably not broad enough a coalition.*
>
> Bernice Reagon, singer

> *—True community begins when we learn to say WE and each day we mean one more.*
>
> Marge Piercy, poet

> *—Community means dealing with some of the people you least want to be with.*
>
> Joanna Macy, Buddhist ecofeminist

(5) Fighting Fairly for Impact, not Injury

A house divided against itself will not be able to stand.

Mark 3:25

A bad enemy destroys freedom, a good enemy provides the loving combat through which we can test and refine our values.

Sam Keen

In solid yet evolving religious communities the status quo is constantly challenged. Growth is both disruptive and broadening. It spells change that, in turn, causes anxiety, then precipitates friction. Conflict is not only inevitable in an effective religious community, but also desirable. Healthy turmoil serves to sharpen issues and educe perspectives. In a church where the members feel the organizational structure is tenuous, they will avoid conflict.

Mature, hardy communities tangle for impact or resultant change rather than injury or retaliatory damage. They struggle openly in order to minimize the lying and cruelty that often contaminate church life. Generative congregations pay heed to the wisdom of minister-politician Hosea Ballou who voiced in 1805: "Let brotherly and sisterly love continue. If we have love, no disagreement can do us any harm; but if we have not love, no agreement can do us any good!"

(6) Generating a Balanced Program

Our mission is to be a redemptive community wherein personal growth, social action, and spiritual awakening are affirmed in word and deed. Congregations fall into disequilibrium when centering upon only one or two dimensions of the comprehensive religious life rather than saluting all three areas simultaneously. It is the job of the politician-minister to be attentive to balancing program life. Nary a business meeting, study group, action effort, or worship experience should transpire in our local temples without participants knowing that they belong to an enterprise that juggles the personal, social, and spiritual dimensions of the robust religious journey.

(7) Producing Where Planted

Someone has sagely noted: "We are called to tend and mend that portion of the cosmic web where we're planted." It is so tempting to spread compassion abroad in the larger world while failing to do so in our home parishes, let alone our very domiciles.

Clergy cannot have a spiritual center in our lives without having a geographical one. We cannot discover who we really are without surrendering fully to where we are. Our local congregation is not a way station but our tilling ground, our sacred ground, our battleground, our growing ground and to be treated as such.

(8) Taking Stewardship Seriously

The minister is called to be an exemplary steward, literally, a "keeper of the hall." If the minister isn't a rugged institutionalist concerned about conserving the resources, maintaining the buildings, shoring up the program life of the local parish, they can hardly expect laity to follow suit. Someone has said: "The church is too important to be left in the hands of the laity." Another person countered: "The church is too important to be left in the hands of the clergy." I say: "An empowering religious faith is too important to be left, period. And to be fulfilled it requires the full-blown leadership of both pulpit and pew."

Survey after survey has shown that administration ranks the lowest among the tasks most enjoyed by clergy. We moan about being either bored or inundated with administrivia. But it is precisely ministering to things and tasks that creates the conditions under which we can preach, pastor, and prophesy. Unless clergy are politically stable and savvy, our overall ministry will wear down, maybe unravel.

Ministers frequently deem certain jobs as beneath them, yet God resides in the mundane stuff and moments of existence. Follow the advice of the Russian author Nabokov to "caress the details, the sacred details." No chore is too insignificant to heed in building the church body politic. We ministers can agonize over and bluster about life's imponderables, oblivious to the fact that most answers lie concealed in the rubble of ordinary existence.

There are three arenas of involvement that uniformly spell the downfall of ministers: **meetings, maintenance, and money**. An astute minister-politician will reframe these challenges in light of the larger principles they underscore. At spiritual core, attending meetings exemplifies the virtue of faithfulness, maintaining buildings enables us to extend beauty, and raising money has everything to do with generosity.

(9) Ever-Evolving

> *We can never be born enough.*
>
> *e.e. cummings*

An expansive religious community is permeable and fluid rather than tight and solidified. It discloses a springy venture, not a static organization. As the radical-wingers of the Protestant Reformation testified in the 16th century: we must be *semper reformanda*, "always reforming, always reforming."

****

COMMUNITY-BUILDING FODDER

It is the capacity for maintenance which is the best test for the vigor and stamina of a society. Any society, church or otherwise, can be galvanized for a while to build something, but the will and skill to keep things in good repair day in, day out are fairly rare.

Eric Hoffer

One of the most vital ways we sustain ourselves is by building communities of resistance, places where we know we are not alone.

bell hooks

Criticism should not be querulous and wasting, all knife and root-puller, but guiding, instructive, inspiring—a south wind, not an east wind.

Ralph Waldo Emerson

Things that matter most must never be at the mercy of things which matter least.

Goethe

ANOTHER BATCH OF MINISTERIAL DRAGONS

• In the midst of ministerial conflicts our tendency is to get bigger—louder, more pompous, pull rank—when what is desirable is to grow small, back off, apologize, spread credit, and share blame. As colleague Makanah Morriss puts it: "If someone is angry or upset with you, first and last, simply listen. Don't match negatives with negatives." After all, our job is not to become the most menacing dragon on the block.

• It is a rare yet ennobling feat for politician-ministers to be essentially the same person privately and publicly. What is our fear here? Congregations don't need to know all the eccentric habits of their religious professionals, but they do hanker for our humanity to shine through consistently.

• One of our pervasive, understandable fears is that we clergy will prove inadequate to this awesome range of ministerial commissions. Well, shake hands with that fear, for there is no way of conquering it!

Judith Walker-Riggs states our dilemma:

> *In our common profession there is no such thing as adequate. For example, when you are with a family whose child has just committed suicide, adequate is bringing the child back to life, but you can't do that. There is no such thing as adequate, there is only learning as much as you can about how to be helpful, and then being there and doing the best you can. But it is never adequate.*

• We clergy generally enter the ministry in order to be liked. We harbor high approval needs. We eschew criticism, failing often to recognize constructive, well-intentioned, censure. We are afraid of rejection, perhaps the scariest dragon of all! What we need to remember about ministry is that we regularly receive accolades and reproach, neither of which we have earned, but that's just the nature of our profession. I take solace in Jack Benny's line: "I don't deserve this award, but I have arthritis, and I don't deserve that either."

One determinant of the health and resiliency of our particular ministry is revealed through our attitude toward detractors and dissenters. Clergy can neither ignore criticism nor be tyrannized by it. The healthiest route is to acknowledge it with simple nods and brief notes.

• We are fearful that we will never recruit another volunteer unless we twist arms that are already far up people's backs. The best way to shake hands with this persistent dragon is by inviting people to fill tasks that meet their needs, match their skills, and will reap recognizable spiritual benefits.

• The Taoist concept of *wu-wei* or effortless action is a healthy antidote to the dragon of perfectionism. Rather than trying to prove our worth—a fruitless endeavor—Taoism encourages clergy not to force things, but instead to roll with the punches, to swim with the current. It encourages relaxed yet focused effort.

MINISTER AS PERSON

TAKING GOOD CARE OF OURSELVES

*W*hen asked how much time a minister ought to spend in meditation, the spiritual leader replied: 'One hour a day, except when you are very, very busy. On those days, meditate two hours.'

Earl Holt

If you fill your calendar with important appointments, you will have no time for God.

If you fill your spare time with essential reading, you will starve your soul.

If you fill your mind with worry about budgets and offerings, the pains in your chest and the ache in your shoulders will betray you. If you try to conform to the expectations of those around you, you will be forever their slave. Work a modest day, then step back and rest. This will keep you close to God.

William Matin

People of the interior life quickly recollect themselves because they never pour forth their whole selves upon outward things.

St. Thomas a Kempis

Every home should have a room, or at least a nook with two chairs, where it is a sin punishable by immediate expulsion to speak of money, business, politics or the state of one's teeth.

Robert Grudin

The clergy's worst sin against the church is not being heretical or unethical, but being just plain dull.

Matthew Fox

How do we find inner peace? We don't. Peace is a gift. We cannot seek it directly. Rather, it is the by-product of living life well.

Will Saunders

Authentic personhood undergirds all other ministerial commissions of pilgrim, philosopher, proclaimer, pastor, prophet, priest, and politician.

A modicum of exhaustion comes with the territory of being a morally sensitive and spiritually keen human being. Yet the gauge for countless hard-driving, high-stepping clergy reads "nearly empty of passion, zest, spirit." Ministers are too often beset with physical depletion, mental fatigue, failure of moral nerve, a cynical mindset, staleness of soul, and severe bouts with self-abuse that breed family neglect as well. Working around the clock to "save the souls" of others, we have failed to develop a sufficient "support system" to cradle our own.

What exacerbates matters is that clergy are all too frequently rewarded for our "workaholism" by both parishioners' accolades and our own driving ambition. In a perverse way, it "pays" to wear ourselves out doing so-called "holy work." Yet self-righteous burnout becomes a degrading way to conclude a noble profession.

Self-care remains our greatest ministerial resource. If we fail to take good, steady care of ourselves, then, sooner or later, our effectiveness will wane. A bleeding heart is of little value to anyone, if it bleeds to death. Rabbi Moshe Leib used to say: "A human being who has not a single hour for their own every day is no human being." Balance is critical for healthy ministry: to work diligently and play joyfully, to give generously and renew constantly. All who labor in the vineyards of mercy and justice should heed that New Testament admonition: "Physician heal thyself!"

Who of us clergy, at death's door, while summing up our lives, would choose to say: "I wish I had attended one more meeting" or "My greatest regret was that I did not spend enough time on temple business?" Instead, our profoundest sadnesses will likely cluster around failing to gaze at enough oceans, take frequent walks in the parks, hold loved ones often and close enough, or visit our interior castles on a daily basis.

The biblical injunction, "Love thy neighbor as thyself" contains an implied equal sign. Ministers can't fully love our neighbors without being at peace with or enjoying ourselves. Such loving requires boundaries. The qualification "as thyself" implies that survival of self is the limit of one's love for one's neighbor. When we don't love ourselves sufficiently, we have little of worth or substance to give to others.

(1) A Tailored Self-Care Regimen

The evidence shows that when ministers are improperly nourished at core levels of our beings, then destructive behavior more likely ensues. Additionally, it is well-nigh impossible to be agents of a life-affirming, hopeful gospel when we ourselves are despondent and dragging our anchors.

Every minister must address the following ticklish query: Does my behavior furnish a positive or negative self-care example for parishioners to emulate in our shared ministry? Like it or not, religious professionals are role models. Our personal lives should underscore our professional ones. We must resemble our resolutions.

Remember there is no magical mixture of physical and spiritual rejuvenation that will fit every minister. We must locate the plan that suits our own psyche and pace.

(2) Regular Sabbaths

Vacation is integral to sustaining a healthy vocational existence.

Vacation entails vacating our minds and our duties. Clergy often hold ambivalence toward holidays, because we are steeped in the puritan ethic that causes considerable unease with "being lazy in all good conscience." Workaholic parsons only transfer our compulsions to new locales. We lug our briefcases to the Bahamas. I confess to working on this book during some of the idle moments during one holiday period. Yet I know well that my vacations are far more renewing when I allow myself to be engrossed in walks, loafing, jigsaw puzzles, and what the monks call "deliberate irrelevancies."

After a frenzied start in ministry where I seldom took a day off, Carolyn and I now regularly take Wednesdays off. It has been a judicious decision, since it grants us a true rest in the middle of the fray, after late Tuesday night meetings and before re-engaging the program load at the end of the week. On our Wednesday sabbath, we enjoy moments alone as well as time together. We bask in massage, strolls, reading, movies, and our grandson. The church has grown to respect our hallowed day-off, primarily because we ourselves have honored it. Moreover, parishioners are no dummies; they receive higher-quality ministry when their professionals are fresher. Buddhist activist Thich Nhat Hanh took Thursdays off even during the period when the South Vietnamese government was trying to suppress the peace movement in which he was deeply involved. "Sir, they are raiding your office and taking your papers!" Hanh replied: "It's Thursday, I will see to it tomorrow!"

As we clergy take regular days off, continuing education breaks, and sabbaticals, we must support laity receiving respites as well. Sometimes our best lay workers become addicted to volunteering within the temple and need to be reminded to take much-needed rest periods. Everyone can benefit from sabbath time-away from the "doings" of their beloved community. We are all irreplaceable, but no one is indispensable, laity or clergy.

(3) Avocations

> *But yield who will to their separation, my object in living is to unite my avocation and my vocation as my two eyes make one in sight. Only where love and need are one, and the work is pay for mortal stakes, is the deed ever really done for Heaven and the future's sakes.*
>
> *Robert Frost*

As my friend remarks: "In ministry, little in your life is lost. Blessedly it can pretty much all be used." I have found that to be true as well. So many of my avocational interests are ingeniously woven into the fabric of my ministry—my guitar playing, my passion for reading and writing, my inveterate enthusiasm for collecting quotes, jokes, and stories, my fascination with fussing over ideas and engaging in serious conversation.

Odd pieces of time are utilized as my roving homiletical eye vacuums up sermon ideas and quotes during my daily reading of newspapers, magazines, or books of any sort. Many life experiences, both delights and travesties, can be explicated beneficially during the course of one's professional journey.

(4) Presence of Sufficient Stress

Balanced ministry exhorts us to embrace *eu-stress* (creative tension), and expel *dis-stress* (debilitating strains). There must be adequate tension in the violin strings to make pleasing music. The same rule obtains in ministry. "Peace and unrest, unrest and peace" is the constant prayerful refrain of clergy.

Caution: "Stress, in addition to being itself, and the result of itself, is also the cause of itself." Whew! Consequently, we dare not be harried or hassled by the very spiritual disciplines we pursue to refresh ourselves. It is smart to heed the Zen Buddhist counsel: "Hasten slowly!"

Someone once inquired of a Zen roshi, who seemed to exude peacefulness no matter what pressures he faced, "How do you maintain such serenity?" He replied, "I never leave my place of meditation!" The roshi meditated early in the morning, and for the rest of the day carried the peace of those moments with him in his mind and heart.

(5) Pruning the Pastoral Schedule

Every pastor's agenda becomes overgrown and needs to be mowed or at least weeded out on a continuing basis.

Clergy are beguiled by the ministerial dragon that if we personally don't do something, then it won't get done. Occasionally that's true, and we must simply let things go or die. But, sometimes, when ministers fail to step in and accomplish a task, if it's crucial enough, congregants will find a way to do the work.

Hardy ministry consists of the reciprocal rhythm of giving and receiving. It is always advantageous for an overall religious community when the paid clergy permit volunteer laity to do things directly for us, beside us, and without us! Ministry is effective when professionals do what we can uniquely do and recommend laity for those jobs that they can singularly do or do as well as ourselves.

A corollary: Always have a good excuse for everything. Clergy are tyrannized by the ethic that "an excuse is a neglect of duty," whereas, in truth, an excuse that has validity helps clarify what our duty is and is not. I recall a layperson phoning me awhile back to cancel a promise he had made to me. He was very nervous and apologetic. What he did not know was that I had been contemplating using my own perfect excuse to cancel myself. I had to reassure him several times that he was doing me a great favor!

(6) Shepherding Our Whole Beings

Clergy must be ready and willing to replenish our soul through silent retreats, refuel our mind through continuing education, recreate our body though "temple maintenance," renew our relational life through support groups and professional counseling, and reform society through well-chosen deeds. These pursuits are mutually reinforcing in the creation of balanced ministerial self-care. And whereas longer lives cannot be promised as a result of rigorous self-care, fuller ones can.

Everyday we are commissioned to nourish with healthful nutrients each zone of our entire person: body, spirit, soul, heart, mind, and conscience. The following abbreviated self-care flow chart is one conceptualized sketch of personal reminders. My selected categories of selfhood are not ranked a la Maslow, and certain activities such as music, sexuality, or laughter assuredly nourish all realms of our being. Each minister will generate additions and corrections to my minutes for her or his own welfare. It is a matter of personal predilection precisely how we feed ourselves; what remains mandatory is that no area be neglected.

BODY

Mr. Duffy lived a few blocks away from his body.
James Joyce

It's not that I'm against exercise. It's just that when I look at my body, I feel it's already been punished enough.

Bob Orben

Great ideas originate in the muscles.
Thomas Edison

We human creatures are *embodied* beings, and our fleshiness transmits profound wisdom to our beings, if we would stop and pay attention. For human fulfillment, we must first be good field animals who move about playfully in the open spaces of the natural world.

Body theology must be a growing concern of both pulpit and pew wherein we: (1) Take care of our body through proper diet, nutrition, and exercise; (2) Engage in "self-massage," that is, lightly and lovingly caressing our own skin for several minutes every day; (3) Honor mutually respectful love as the central principle in sexual sharing with our chosen partner; and (4) Relate to the earth and all its inhabitants as one body to another.

SPIRIT

Blessed are they who are at home in the Spirit.
New Testament beatitude

How goes it with thy Spirit?
Quaker greeting

Spiritual work entails the cultivation of an evolving mystical consciousness where one's inner spirit (Atman) draws strength from and reconnects with the God-head (Brahman). At bedrock, the spiritual journey begins with attentiveness to inhaling and exhaling. My simplest breathing exercise is joined with these words by Thich Nhat Hanh: "Breathing in, I calm my body and mind. Breathing out, I smile. Dwelling in the present moment, I know this is the only moment."

Spirit activities include meditation and prayer, music and chanting, while immersing oneself amid the classic spiritual questions: Who am I (identity)? Whose am I (affiliation)? Where am I going (destination)? and With whom might I travel (companionship)?

My favorite daily chant repeats the Hindu phrase, **Om Nama Shivaya** that roughly translates: "I honor the divinity I meet within..." Hindis chant this for days on end; fifteen minutes suffices to center my being and brace me for the day ahead. As much as I enjoy singing, alone and with others, I have grown especially fond of chants. They are simple, circular, repetitious, and utterly sharable whether walking, commuting by car, or sitting quietly in one's office.

SOUL

Whereas spirit work has to do with sailing the skies and connecting with the transcendent, soul-work focuses on tilling the soil and "raking the ashes." Jungian analyst James Hillman makes sharp distinctions between the life of the spirit that centers upon peaks, heat, and ascent and the soul that centers upon valleys, moisture, and descent. Soul also represents, for me, engaging the shadowed dimensions of existence, in particular anger, anguish, and angst.

Like Adam, we were not fashioned out of light or fire but mud. Our ancestral home is grounded in the earth. Our humaneness, our humility, and our humor are based in the humus of our origins. We are like trees having a remarkable ability to grow both up and down at the same time, with its huge panoply of branches above, its unseen but vast system of roots below, and its trunk (symbolizing the soul) linking and separating these two complex networks. We religious questors can and must grow up and down at the same time.

HEART

Does this path have a heart?

Carlos Casteneda

Your heart is not living until it has experienced pain...The pain of love breaks open the heart, even if it is as hard as a rock.

Hazrat Inayat Khan

The heart refers to our deep-down inner feelings of sympathy, compassion, understanding, and trust. As ministers we are ever reminded to be open-hearted, strong-hearted, clear-hearted, and full-hearted as we challenge ourselves and parishioners to foster the primary loves of life: self, neighbor, nature, and God. The *heart* of our religious philosophy must always reside in the *hearths* where we live, move, and have our being. A vibrant, vital faith is brought home to the places and encounters of our daily existence.

We are challenged personally and professionally to be courageous (from the French *coeur* for "heart"). Courageous leaders both confront the heartless and lift the disheartened of society.

MIND

If I go to heaven, I want to take my reason with me.

Robert Ingersoll

Where is the Life we have lost in living? Where is the wisdom we have lost in knowledge? Where is the knowledge we have lost in information?

T. S. Eliot

As mindful beings, ministers are dedicated to evolving from information-gatherers to wisdom-sharers on the quest to becoming sages (not saints). We are commissioned to forge a reasonable faith. Toward that end, I stretch my mental capacities by keeping a journal, reading viewpoints with which I disagree, and reciting short poems.

I combined my passions for reading and writing years ago through composing daily devotions for myself, then for others, to enjoy. Along with the Psalmist, I believe that those of us who read or create daily meditation manuals "shall be like trees planted by the rivers of water."

CONSCIENCE

Service is the rent we pay for living on earth.

Alice Walker

Sometimes our conscience takes up more room than all the rest of our insides.

Mark Twain

Today's surgeons can transplant hearts, kidneys, and other human organs, but no man or woman in the health sciences can yet transplant a conscience. Feed and care for your conscience as you do your brain; neither can be replaced.

Stephen Fritchman

I believe that the religious mission is to become "freethinking mystics with hands." Our inner work must produce hands outstretched in praise and service. As ministers we must shun convenient consciences that would have us do only what is easy and nearby and, instead, grow mature consciences that venture expansive, costly efforts of compassion.

I close this section with the story that the Rabbi of Zans used to tell about himself:

> *In my youth when I was fired with the love of God, I thought I would convert the whole world to God. But soon I discovered that it would be quite enough to convert the people who lived in my town, and I tried for a long time, but did not succeed. Then I realized that my program was still much too ambitious, and I concentrated on the persons in my own household. But I could not convert them either. Finally it dawned on me I must work upon myself, so that I may give true service to God. But I did not accomplish even this.*

We ministers won't accomplish full self-renewal, but staying on course keeps us awake and faithful to our vision.

LOVE MEETS THE DRAGONS

*T*here is no fear in love, but perfect love casts out fear.

I John 4:18

Embrace fear. Invite it into the house of awareness. Hold it gently until it is ready to leave. Push fears out the front door, disown them or try to conquer them by will power and they will only return by the back door, like rejected children seeking love. I am the parent of my fears; they will only depart when I have learned to accept them.

Sam Keen

You gain strength, courage and confidence by every experience in which you really stop to look fear in the face.

Eleanor Roosevelt

When the people of Israel were waiting on the banks of the Jordan River to enter the Promised Land, God told Joshua to tell the priests: 'Lift up the Ark of Covenant and pass in front of the people...Tell them that when they come to the edge of the waters of the Jordan, they are to take their stand in the river.'

Joshua 3: 6, 8

We must accept finite disappointment, but we must never lose infinite hope.

Martin Luther King, Jr.

If during our ministries we know not perfect love, it is equally true that we cannot tolerate absolute fear. As John MacNeil put it: "Perfect fear casts out all love and generates self-hatred," and might well have added, ruins ministries. If we are swallowed up by the dragons, all will be in vain.

Yet a ministry unencumbered by fears would be boring and stagnant, without challenge or juice; it could even prove reckless. In the epic American saga, *Moby Dick*, the chief mate Starbuck says to his crew: "I will have no person in my boat who is not afraid of a whale." Melville goes on to say:

> By this Starbuck seemed to mean not only was the most reliable and useful courage that which arises from the fair estimation of the encountered peril, but that an utterly fearless person is a far more dangerous comrade than a coward.

Fear is the finger pointing out where the problem is—if we go in the direction of fear, it will push us toward growth. As one writer put it, "hug your monsters," for as long as we run away from our conflicts, they will harass us wherever we go.

Such counsel pertains to ministry as well. There must be a realistic reckoning with the adversaries in our professional encounters. Being brave does not mean being foolhardy or taking stupid risks with precious things. The dragons of ministry cannot be ignored, denied, or wished out of existence. They cannot be suppressed or seduced. They must be faced.

The Old Testament unequivocally states that "fear of God is the beginning of wisdom" (Psalm 111:10). **Beginning** is the critical term, but awe-filled (not craven) fear is present nonetheless. As Martin Buber writes:

> Those who begin with the love of God without having previously experienced the fear of God, love an idol that they have made, a god whom it is easy enough to love. They do not love the real God who is, to begin with, dreadful and incomprehensible.

It may appear odd to say that God is to be feared. Dragons yes, life yes, but God? The Eternal Spirit should admittedly be revered, but held in dread? In the Qur'an the word *takwa* is often translated as "fear" but could better be interpreted as vigilance, veneration, even god-consciousness. In any case, in the presence of God, it is proper that we ministers should remain vigilant, afraid, cautious not to offend, on edge, full of awe.

Fear is a valuable sensibility in dealing with the divine as well as useful in incarnating ministry. Who would want to be operated upon by a surgeon who never feared that he or she might make a mistake? Who would want to be transported by a nonchalant airplane pilot? Who would want to be ceremonialized by a minister who was void of nervous strain? I always tell couples preparing to join their lives in holy union that I expect them, as well as myself, to be duly anxious in the light of their forthcoming ceremony—panicky, no...tense, yes. Feeling fear enables us to be more fully present. Fear spells awareness: awareness of danger and opportunities, of limitations and promise.

One of the medieval scholastics wrote: "Work, therefore, in what you do, from love and not from fear." In truth, we ought to work from both love and fear, for each in its own way is a prime motivator. As clergy, we are prone to suppress our fears, but in so doing we also banish courage, freedom, and creativity. Our anxious sensitivities keep our ministries awake and quivering, less prone to grow stodgy or smug. The Bible warns us all to "work out our salvation with fear and trembling!" We need dragons, they are our cohorts. Remember as Rumi stated: "Our greatest fears are like dragons guarding our greatest treasures." If we slay them, the priceless assets and abundance of our profession will lie unprotected.

Since I have yet to encounter a live dragon, let me give an example about a real tiger. The same point prevails.

A colleague was standing in front of the tiger area in a

world-famous Zoo. There were several people beside Ted. The huge beast singled out one person next to him and stared straight at this woman, while emitting a low growl. After this had gone on for some time, Ted remarked to the woman: "Doesn't that shake you to have the tiger glare at you that way? The tiger seems to have it in for you." She replied: "No, for several years I was its keeper and fed it everyday. It knows me and talks to me."

I have thought back on that incident often, as a kind of parable of the soul. What was giving my ministerial friend imaginary terror was, for the woman who knew her tiger, a message of affection. It was a real beast, a savage animal and could have torn Ted to shreds except for the gap between them, but because this woman knew and understood it, and also had a healthy respect for its power, it was quite a different animal. That woman knew her tiger.

Each of us possesses a private tiger within our souls. We conceal aggressive impulses that are capable of healing or destroying. We need to recognize our private tiger is growling and on the prowl. We need to own our tiger, to be in amicable, regular touch with it, just like shaking hands with the dragons.

It is our ministerial responsibility to acknowledge, honor, know our dragons. In fact, over the long haul, those ministers who neither run from nor fight their fears but face them with courage are invariably the most satisfied and satisfying professionals.

EPILOGUE

Perhaps all the dragons in our lives are princesses who are only waiting to see us act, just once, with beauty and courage. Perhaps everything that frightens us is, in its deepest essence, something helpless that wants our love.

Rainer Maria Rilke

Universalism is not faith in the inevitability of heaven which supports me as I face death but faith in the reality of love. The old Universalist heresy claimed that God's love knew no limits and would find the sinner no matter how far from holiness she or he strayed. The fundamental nature of reality is love.

Gordon McKeeman

In the end, ministry is deceptively simple. We tend not to trust the simplicity at the heart of religion, that we were made by love and for love.

Alan Jones

Nothing in all creation can separate us from the love of God...

Romans 8: 39

My ministry has been grounded in and sustained by the embrace of Eternal Love. The universalist conception of God's love is clear: We were created by a loving God, we are buoyed by that same transforming power along life's pathway, and we will ultimately return to its kindly, tender grasp. As Paul puts it: "Love will never come to an end."

Ministry is a human vocation that ingests the fullness of God's love, then dares to spread that love abroad through its various commissions of the pilgrim, the philosopher, the proclaimer, the pastor, the prophet, the priest, the politician, and the person. As ministers our all-encompassing mission is to ensoul Fyodor Dostoevsky's admonition:

> Love all God's creation, the whole of it and every grain of sand. Love every leaf and every ray of God's light. Love the animals, love the plants, love everything. If you love everything you will perceive the divine mystery in all things.

Through ministry, love meets head on the most inescapable and insidious of human fears. During the course of our professional journey, we will neither experience nor embody perfect love. It is an unrealizable earthly ideal. Our ministries are perpetually visited by dragons with which we must gracefully learn to shake hands.

Then, at the close of our vocational tenure, we release the outcomes and return our singular contributions to the flow of history. And at the conclusion of our earthly lives, we surrender our bodies and spirits to a loving God. St. John of the Cross wrote: "In the end we shall be examined in love." Not only examined in love, but moreover, embraced with love.

As religious pilgrims we know not the exact nature of our tomorrows but we fear not. We can rest assured. If during our lifetimes the dragons are occasionally embraced, in eternity perhaps they will be transformed into our dance partners in the everlasting gambol of Love.

MAIL ORDER INFORMATION

For additional copies of *Love Meets the Dragons,* send $12.95 plus $2.00 per book for shipping and handling (California residents add 7 $3/_4$% sales tax.) Make checks payable to the author and mail to: Tom Owen-Towle, 3303 Second Avenue, San Diego, CA 92103.

Also available through local bookstores that use R. R. Bowker Company Books in Print catalogue system. For bookstore discount, order through the publisher, SunInk Publications, formerly Sunflower Ink Publishing.